Letters
from
Korean
History

Notes on the English translation

Korean personal names, place names, proper nouns and common nouns have been transliterated according to the Revised Romanization of Korean system, introduced by the South Korean government in 2000. The only exceptions are names that are widely recognized in other forms, such as Syngman Rhee (Lee Seungman) or Kim Ilsung (Kim Ilseong). Two of the most common Korean surnames, Kim and Park, have been left in their conventional forms, rather than Gim and Bak (which would be their spellings according to the Revised Romanization system). The surname Lee, meanwhile, is transliterated as Yi before 1945, in accordance with convention (for example, Yi Seonggye), and then in the more modern form of Lee after 1945, taking Korean liberation as a somewhat arbitrary dividing line. Surnames are listed before first names, in the Korean style, with the singular, Americanized exception of Syngman Rhee.

The ages of individuals are listed in accordance with the original Korean text of *Letters from Korean History*, which naturally follows the Korean convention for age calculation. This means that figures given are generally one year higher than what would be considered the corresponding "Western" age.

Letters from Korean History

5

From the Daehan Empire to North-South rapprochement

Park Eunbong

CUM LIBRO 책과함께

History in Northeast Asia is like a minefield. Riddled with unresolved issues, controversies, disputed territory and conflicting ideologies, it often breeds acrimony among governments and peoples in the region. Within many countries, too, blind nationalism, political bias and censorship constantly threaten to distort the picture painted by historians of their country's past and, by extension, present. Creating a balanced narrative in the midst of such tension and conflicting perspectives is no easy task. But that is what Park Eunbong appears to have done in *Letters from Korean History*.

Offering children and young readers an unbiased version of their past is one of the kindest and most responsible ways of helping them grow into broad-minded citizens, capable of sustaining peace and cooperation in a region - and world - that grows more interconnected every year but still bears unhealed historical scars and bruises. In Korea, such a history also offers context that can put the country's current state of division - only sixty-seven years old as of 2015 - into wider perspective.

Making any Korean book accessible to readers of English through translation is a privilege. The same goes for *Letters from Korean History*. In a series of letters addressed to a young reader overseas, the author adopts a conversational style of writing that conveys the ups and downs, ins and outs of Korean history with ease. But while the language is highly accessible, the content is never rendered simplistic or patronizing, and issues that lose some other historians in a fog of

nationalism are navigated by Park with the kind of healthy detachment and clarity that inspires confidence in the reader.

Progressing from the stones and bones of prehistory all the way to the turbulent twentieth century in the course of five volumes, *Letters from Korean History* can be browsed as a reference text or plowed through from beginning to end. As with most histories that cover such a long period, the density of information increases as the narrative approaches the present. The relatively recent Joseon period, for example, accounts for two of the five volumes (III and IV), rich as it is in events and meticulously recorded historical data.

Letters from Korean History has been a great success in its native country among Korean readers. I hope that this translation will now be of help to ethnic Koreans overseas, others interested in Korea or history in general, Koreans looking to study history and English at the same time, and anybody else who believes that exploring the past is a good way to try and make sense of the confusing, flawed and wonderful present.

Ben Jackson
May, 2016

To readers of 'Letters from Korean History'

Letters from Korean History is a series of some seventy letters covering a period that stretches from prehistory to the present. Unlike most introductions to Korean history, it takes a theme-based approach: each theme functions as a window onto a particular period. The use of several different windows offering various perspectives onto the same period is meant to help the reader form her or his own more complete picture of that part of history. For example, "Buddhism, key to the culture of the Three Kingdoms" and "Silla, land of the bone-rank system," two letters in Volume I, offer two different ways of understanding Silla history: a religious perspective via Buddhism; and a social caste-based perspective by way of the bone-rank system. My hope is that, after reading both letters and exploring these two separate approaches, readers will come closer to gaining a comprehensive understanding of Silla. The more diverse the windows opened, the more helpful this should be in the forming of a complete image.

Letters from Korean History places equal emphasis on aspects such as culture, everyday life, society and social segments with habitually low historical profiles, such as women and children. This is an important difference to conventional introductory histories, which naturally tend towards narratives centered on ruling classes by prioritizing political history.

I have also attempted to portray Korean history not as that of a single nation in isolation but as part of world history as a whole, and to adopt a perspective that places humans as just one species in the universe and nature. This is why the first letter begins not with prehistory on the Korean Peninsula but with the birth of the human race on Earth. The connection with world history is maintained throughout the five volumes, in which Korea's interactions, relationships and

points of comparison with the rest of the world are constantly explored.

The single most distinct aspect of *Letters from Korean History* is that, unlike most general histories, which make passing references to characters and dates, it depicts Korea's past through a series of engaging stories. It is my hope that these will help readers feel like direct witnesses to historical scenes as they unfold. All content is based on historical materials, either in their original form or adapted without distortion. Sources include key texts such as *Samguk sagi* ("History of the Three Kingdoms"), *Samguk yusa* ("Memorabilia of the Three Kingdoms"), Goryeosa ("History of Goryeo") and *Joseon wangjo sillok* ("Royal Annals of the Joseon Dynasty"), as well as a variety of literary anthologies, letters, journals and epigraphs.

The English version of *Letters from Korean History* is published for young readers overseas who are curious about Korea and its people, and for young Korean readers keen to learn more about their own history while improving their language skills as global citizens. I hope that readers will not feel obliged to start at the beginning of Volume I and plow all the way through; rather, each letter contains a historical episode in its own right, and can be chosen and read according to the reader's particular area of interest. The text is complemented by plenty of photos and illustrations, giving a more vivid sense of history - reading the captions that accompany these should enhance the sense of historical exploration.

I very much hope that this book will become a useful source of guidance for young readers, wherever they may be.

Park Eunbong

May, 2016

Contents

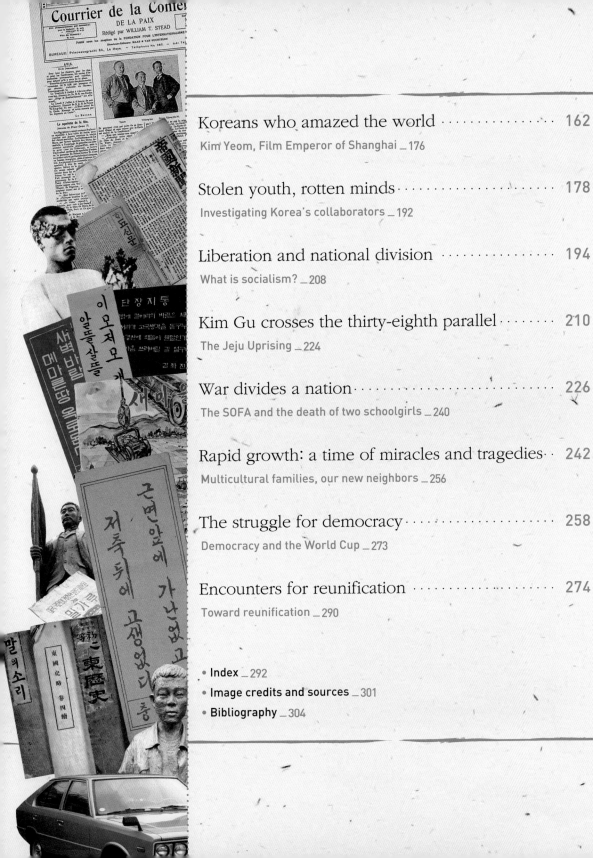

CHAPTER 1

Lost sovereignty

The Protectorate Treaty was thus signed at around two o'clock in the morning on November 18, 1905.

The treaty was signed unilaterally and by force, leaving Japan in control of the foreign affairs of the Daehan Empire. So how on earth did the empire get itself into such a helpless position?

TIME
LINE

1905

Daehan Empire

Protectorate Treaty
signed under duress

1907

Daehan Empire

national debt
redemption movement

1909

Daehan Empire

An Junggeun shoots Ito
Hirobumi in Harbin

Many Koreans of your age grew up hearing from their grandparents about the time when Japan ruled Korea. Back then, they had to speak Japanese at school and their teachers came from Japan.

This time, known as the colonial period, is one of the most painful episodes in Korean history. But how did it happen - how did one country come to oppress another?

By the early twentieth century, many countries had become colonies of the Great Powers. Hegemonic states such as Britain, France, Germany and the United States had colonized places including India, Vietnam, Indonesia and the Philippines in Asia, not to mention large swathes of Africa. But the Daehan Empire became a colony of a fellow Asian state: its own neighbor, in fact. Japan had opened its doors to the outside world and begun embracing Western culture some twenty years earlier. From then on it had undergone a rapid transformation and was soon eyeing up the Korean Peninsula, ready to join the other Great Powers in the colonization game.

Today, let's see exactly how Korea ended up losing its sovereignty to Japan.

1919	1920	1923	1923
Colonial period	Colonial period	Colonial period	Colonial period
March First Movement	Kim Jwajin wins Battle of Qingshanli	Bang Jeonghwan establishes Children's Day	Kanto Massacre takes place in Japan

Have you ever heard of the Protectorate Treaty? Japan forced the Daehan Empire to sign this agreement, which was the first step towards colonization, in 1905. Let's have a look at the circumstances leading up to the signing.

Japan sent Ito Hirobumi, one of its leading politicians, to Joseon to oversee the signing of the Protectorate Treaty. You may well have heard of Ito, as he was later assassinated by Korean patriot An Junggeun. To Koreans, Ito is a symbol of colonial aggression, but Japanese know him as a famous politician. He played a leading role in introducing Western culture to Japan, created the country's constitution and served no fewer than four times as its prime minister. But the story of his assassination is for later on - in this

Jungmyeongjeon Hall
The Protectorate Treaty was signed in this building, designed by a Russian architect in 1900. It still stands in Seoul's Jeong-dong neighborhood, though this photo was taken during the colonial period. The hall once lay within the grounds of Gyeongungung Palace (known today as Deoksugung), but found itself outside them when the size of the palace was drastically reduced. The palace's current name comes from "Deoksu," a name given to Gojong by the Japanese—it was in this palace that the former emperor lived at the time.

letter, I want to focus on the Protectorate Treaty. Ito arrived in the Daehan Empire on November 9, 1905.

The Protectorate Treaty: Korea loses control of its own foreign affairs

Upon arriving in Korea, Ito Hirobumi met Gojong.

"Your Majesty, the Japanese Empire intends to manage the foreign affairs of Joseon. This is for the wellbeing and protection of you and your country……. Whether or not you give consent for this is up to you. If you refuse, however, you must consider what the outcome of your decision will be, given that the government of the Japanese Empire has already made up its own mind. You will have to prepare for an outcome less favorable than signing this treaty."

Ito's tone was respectful, but his words amounted to pure blackmail: Joseon had better sign a treaty transferring control of its foreign affairs to Japan, or else. Such control, of course, is highly important in that it allows states to interact with each other on an equal basis. It is, in other words, a symbol of independence; as such, losing it meant that Joseon would forfeit its national autonomy and be subject to constant interference and control by Japan. When Ito talked about the wellbeing and protection of Joseon, he meant making Japan's neighbor into little more than a puppet with no control of

Ito Hirobumi
Ito traveled to the Daehan Empire to ensure the signing of the Protectorate Treaty.

The Meiji Restoration
This event of 1868 brought huge change to Japan. The country introduced laws and systems like those of the Western powers and rapidly developed its industries, then transformed into an imperial power as it sought the raw materials and markets needed for continued industrial growth. Meiji was the name of the Japanese emperor at the time. Ito Hirobumi was one of the leading figures behind the restoration.

its own foreign affairs.

Gojong resisted Ito's attempt at blackmail, but to no avail. The next day, Japanese soldiers and policemen took up positions in and around the palace and at other points in the Joseon capital. Ito gathered the country's ministers and demanded that they agree to the treaty. While most of them hesitated, minister of education Yi Wanyong spoke up.

"I think we have no choice but to meet Japan's demands. Japan has made many sacrifices to defend Joseon during the two wars it fought against Qing and Russia. And Joseon's diplomacy so far has disturbed the peace in East Asia and led Joseon itself into crisis. Given the circumstances, Japan's suggestion of this treaty is inevitable."

Yi sounded more like a Japanese minister than a leading member of the Korean government. His words enraged prime minister Han Gyuseol.

"No! I'll never agree! Signing this treaty would mean the end of Joseon!"

Ito now lost his temper.

"Just think good and hard about your decision! And don't forget that this treaty has to be signed. There's no telling what the consequences might be if you ignore our demands."

In the end, minister of foreign affairs Park Jesun, minister

Gojong in imperial uniform
After proclaiming the Daehan Empire in 1897, Gojong adopted a Western-style imperial costume.

Yi Wanyong and Han Gyuseol
Yi was the primary advocate of signing the Protectorate Treaty, while Han was expelled from the meeting room when he opposed it. Today, Yi is reviled as a pro-Japanese traitor and Han is held up as a patriot.

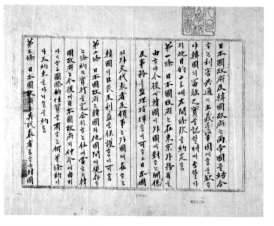

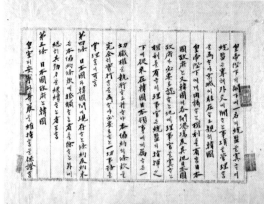

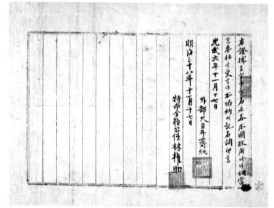

Text of the Protectorate Treaty
This treaty stipulated that the Daehan Empire could not sign any treaty with another state without the permission of Japan, and that the latter would deal with the Daehan Empire's foreign affairs. Nowhere is there any evidence that Gojong approved the treaty. –Independence Hall of Korea

of home affairs Yi Jiyong, minister of education Yi Wanyong and minister of defense Yi Geuntaek agreed to the treaty, while prime minister Han Gyuseol and minister of finance Min Yeonggi opposed it. Minister of agriculture, commerce and industry Gwon Junghyeon, meanwhile, initially opposed the treaty but later changed his mind.

Ito took Park Jesun's seal and used it to stamp the treaty documents. In Joseon, nobody had the right to use the seal

The Protectorate Treaty is signed by force
Ito Hirobumi gathered the Daehan Empire's
ministers and instructed them to agree
to the treaty. Eventually, Ito took foreign
minister Park Jesun's official seal and
stamped the treaty document himself.

without the permission of Gojong himself, but Ito didn't care.
The Protectorate Treaty was thus signed at around two o'clock
in the morning on November 18, 1905.

The treaty was signed unilaterally and by force, leaving
Japan in control of the foreign affairs of the Daehan Empire.
So how on earth did the empire get itself into such a helpless
position?

Caught in the machinations of the Great Powers

Though Korea was officially known as the Daehan Empire at
the time the Protectorate Treaty was signed, it did not possess
the power that its grandiose name implied and was unable to
stop Japan. To make matters worse, the international climate
was rapidly changing to the latter's advantage. Western

The Russo-Japanese War
This conflict was instigated by Japan in February, 1904, and ended in victory for the aggressor in July of the following year. Japan forced the Daehan Empire to sign the Protectorate Treaty barely two months later. This illustration, published in a French newspaper at the time, shows a battle between Japan and Russia at Jeongju in Pyeongan-do Province.

Imperialism
The period from the late-nineteenth to early-twentieth century is known as the "age of imperialism." The Great Powers colonized and forcibly ruled countries that offered markets for the goods they produced and sources of the raw materials needed by their industries. Some of the leading empires were those of Britain, France, Germany, Italy, Russia and Japan. They competed among themselves to acquire more colonies, engaging in an ongoing series of wars.

powers such as the United States and Britain began siding with Korea's eastern neighbor, in order to prevent Russia from acquiring too much power in Asia.

Japan was able to force the Protectorate Treaty upon the Daehan Empire at will because the United States and Britain turned a blind eye to its ambitions. Each of the two Western powers had given Japan its explicit support, in the form of the Taft-Katsura Secret Agreement and the second Anglo-Japanese Alliance, respectively.

The Taft-Katsura Secret Agreement was reached by American secretary of war William Howard Taft and Japanese prime minister Katsura Taro in July 1905, while the Russo-Japanese War was still in progress. The two politicians agreed that Japan would rule the Daehan Empire and the United States would govern the Philippines. The text of the second Anglo-Japanese Alliance, meanwhile, recognized that Japan would make the Daehan Empire its protectorate. Such agreements may seem ludicrous now, but they were reached during the so-called imperial age, when the world's great powers were in the habit of carving up weaker countries among themselves for their own profit.

With victory over Russia and the agreement of the US and Britain, Japan was unstoppable. Triumphantly, it railroaded the Protectorate Treaty and snapped up the Daehan Empire for itself. So you could say the colonization of the empire resulted from conflicts of interest among the Western powers, since they effectively handed it over to Japan to serve their own interests. Though the biggest problem, of course, was the Daehan Empire's failure to build up the strength to survive in this environment.

Lost sovereignty and a dethroned emperor

Once the Protectorate Treaty was signed, Japan steadily prepared for full colonization of the Daehan Empire. After using the Hague incident(see page 26) as a pretext to strip Gojong of his title as emperor, it put his son, Sunjong, on the throne to serve as a mere

Disarmed Daehan troops
In 1907, Japan forced Gojong to abdicate as emperor and disbanded the Daehan imperial army.

Park Seunghwan
When Japan gave the order to disband the Daehan imperial army, commander Park Seung-hwan of the First Regiment took his own life. He left a suicide note that read, "As a soldier I was unable to serve my country; as a subject I was unable to remain loyal to my emperor. I deserve to die ten thousand times."

figurehead. Japan also disbanded the empire's armed forces, the last potential obstacle to total manipulation.

Dissolution came as the final straw to the soldiers of the Daehan Empire, who now rose up and fought against the Japanese army. Their anger was further provoked by the suicide of officer Park Seunghwan. A fierce battle was fought in the middle of Seoul, as described by one witness:

"It had been drizzling since the morning, and the raindrops got heavier as the day passed. All the drains and sewers were overflowing. The sound of gunfire kept on coming through the rain, while everywhere was knee-deep in water. The whole city was gripped by fear. Even more shockingly, the water flowing through the streets was tinged red. The blood of our soldiers mixed with those of the Japanese, till the whole capital was awash with it."

Text of the Treaty of Annexation
Signed on August 22, 1910 and proclaimed a week later, the Treaty of Annexation stipulated that the sovereignty of the Daehan Empire would be transferred completely and in perpetuity to Japan.
–Kyujanggak Institute for Korean Studies

The battle ended with defeat for the soldiers of the Daehan Empire. Their state now had no control over its own foreign affairs and no army. All that was left was the formal signing of a treaty of annexation with Japan.

On August 16, 1910, the Japanese presented Yi Wanyong, who had now risen from the position of education minister to

Koreans awarded peerages by Japan

Japan established the Government-General and proclaimed its intention to rule Joseon. It then awarded peerages to seventy-six Korean officials and members of the royal family in the name of the Japanese emperor. Among those who had agreed to the annexation, Yi Wanyong and Yi Jiyong were made counts and Park Jesun, Gwon Junghyeon and Yi Geuntaek viscounts. Han Gyuseol, who had opposed the Protectorate Treaty, was awarded the title of baron but refused it.

Among the seventy-six Koreans given titles by Japan, some refused by taking their own lives. Others were stripped of their titles when they later campaigned for independence. Most, however, accepted their peerages with resignation. Japan also gave cash handouts to provincial officials and yangban—a trick, of course, to dissuade them from opposing their new colonial master.

Yi Eun, the last crown prince
The short boy in the front row is Yi Eun, the last crown prince of the Daehan Empire. After the annexation, Yi was sent to study in Japan: effectively, he had been taken hostage. He had been due to take Min Gabwan, a Korean, as his wife, but Japan stopped this wedding from going ahead and had him marry Japanese princess Masako (whose Korean name was Yi Bangja).

that of prime minister, with the text of a treaty of annexation. A council of ministers was held two days later, followed by another meeting in the presence of Sunjong on August 22. It was here that the prime minister finally signed the treaty. One week later, on August 29, Sunjong publicly proclaimed the annexation. The Daehan Empire was now a colony of Japan. Today, August 29 is known as "National Humiliation Day," in memory of this shameful episode in Korean history.

Well, that's how the Daehan Empire ended up a colony of Japan. It remained so for thirty-five years, until 1945.

Here comes the 'sunsa!'

After the annexation, Japan tore down several buildings in the grounds of Gyeongbokgung, Joseon's main royal palace, and built the headquarters of the Government-General in their place. The Government-General was the heart and the symbol of Japanese imperialism. The building that housed its headquarters remained standing until 1995, when it was demolished. I vividly remember the sight of its cold, gray stone walls towering incongruously behind Gwanghwamun Gate.

The land survey
Japan passed a law requiring all Joseon farmers to report the land they owned to the government. Though it claimed the law was designed to make land ownership clear and to levy tax on previously unregistered land in a fair manner, its actual aim was to snatch Korean land and rule the country as a colony. This photo shows land being measured as part of the survey.

The Government-General building
This building, the hub of Japanese imperialism, stood in the grounds of Gyeongbokgung Palace, a symbol of Joseon. Look carefully: you'll see that Gwanghwamun and Heungnyemun gates are missing. The latter was completely destroyed, while the former almost suffered the same fate but was rescued by a few conscientious Japanese who had it moved to another location, north of Geonchunmun Gate. After liberation, the Government-General building housed Korean government offices and was later used as the National Museum of Korea. It was destroyed on August 15, 1995.

Gyeongbokgung restored
This photo shows Gwanghwamun and Heungnyemun gates after their restoration and the demolition of the Government-General building. Gwanghwamun was restored after liberation, in 1969, but recently rebuilt again because the position and appearance of the 1969 reconstruction were inaccurate. Heungnyemun was restored in 2001.

All eight of the governor-generals placed in charge of Joseon during the thirty-five years of the colonial period were Japanese military men who ruled the colony by the gun and the sword. The first governor-general, Terauchi Masatake, used notorious Japanese policemen armed with swords to implement a series of colonial policies including a

Colonial education
In front of these students stands a teacher in military uniform and a sword at his side. The colonial authorities taught Japanese language and songs and trained young Koreans to be loyal to Japan, with the aim of making Joseon their colony forever. This kind of practice is known as colonial education. The picture here is by Elizabeth Keith, a British woman who visited Joseon at the time.

comprehensive land survey of the country.

The survey pushed Joseon's peasants even further into poverty and hardship. Japanese citizens acquired large amounts of land, while Koreans became their tenant farmers. Those who couldn't even rent land had to leave their villages or become beggars. Many left in search of new lives in far-flung places such as Manchuria, Primorsky Krai or Siberia.

That was not all. Japan closely monitored and controlled Joseon's villages, companies, factories and even schools. Japanese police, known as *sunsa*, roamed every last corner of the country, watching over and interfering in the lives of the people. If a child cried, its parents would scare it into silence by telling by it the *sunsa* were coming. They were frightening figures. The schoolteachers, meanwhile, would teach in uniform and with swords at their sides. You can imagine how horrible that was.

Secret mission to The Hague

In June 1907, two years after the Protectorate Treaty was signed, three Koreans arrived in The Hague. The emissaries—Yi Sangseol, Yi Jun and Yi Wijong—carried secret orders from Gojong. They had made the long journey to the Netherlands to attend the Second Hague Conference, an international peace conference, where their instructions were to expose Japan's acts of aggression and win back control of foreign policy for the Daehan Empire.

The emissaries arrived at their hotel, unpacked their luggage and set to work. They met conference chairman Count Nelidorf, the Dutch foreign minister and representatives of powers such as the United States, France and Germany, whom they asked for help. But all their attempts met with failure. At the time, the Western powers were on good terms with Japan and had already agreed to its move to make Korea into a protectorate. There was no way they would have listened to what these three men from Joseon had to say. In the end, the

Paper publishes interview with Hague emissary
The July 5, 1907 edition of this French newspaper ran an interview with Yi Sangseol, one of the three emissaries.

emissaries were unable to take part in the conference, but they did have the chance to hold a press conference with several international journalists. Yi Wijong, who spoke several foreign languages, delivered their speech.

The journalists who heard Yi speak felt sorry for Joseon. But that was all: sympathy from the press could do nothing to change the situation. The Hague emissaries had failed in their mission to inform participants at the Second Hague Conference about Joseon's predicament and win back control of their country's foreign affairs. The story about Yi Jun committing suicide by disemboweling himself in anger is untrue: in fact, he died of illness. Still, his death was effectively due to the deep sorrow and anger caused by his country's loss of sovereignty.

Hague emissaries Yi Sangseol, Yi Jun and Yi Wijong
Yi Sangseol had been a senior minister of the second rank in the State Council and spoke good French and English. Yi Wijong was the son of former Russian minister Yi Beomjin and also an outstanding linguist. Yi Jun was a prosecutor and a strong patriot.

CHAPTER 2

The struggle to save the country

Sin Dolseok and his men were warmly welcomed wherever they went, thanks to their consistent victories and the consideration they showed local villagers. Some 300 in number, they fought across a large swathe of the country. Sin built several secret bases in valleys deep within the Taebaek mountains, from which he crossed back and forth over the mountains into Gyeongsang-do Province, Gangwon-do Province and the east coast, ambushing Japanese troops. Sin's uncanny appearances in different places in rapid succession sparked rumors that he was using magic powers to transport himself.

TIME LINE

1905
Daehan Empire
Protectorate Treaty signed
under duress

1907
Daehan Empire
national debt
redemption movement

1909
Daehan Empire
An Junggeun shoots Ito
Hirobumi in Harbin

In my last letter, I talked about the five years from the signing of the Protectorate Treaty to Japan's official annexation of Korea. Hopefully you now understand how Japan came to make the Daehan Empire its colony.

"I'd have fought back against the Japanese," you may say. "Or at least written newspaper articles telling people just how bad Japan was."

Well, that's just what many people did. Some joined righteous armies and fought directly; others wrote in newspapers and magazines to publicize Japan's aggression; still others built schools and tried to enlighten their fellow Koreans, believing education was the key to saving the country, or raised money and tried to pay off Korea's debt to Japan... Their methods may have been different, but all of them shared the same aim: freeing Korea and its people from Japanese oppression.

Today, let's look at some of the movements to save Korea at the time.

1919

Colonial period
March First Movement

1920

Colonial period
Kim Jwajin wins
Battle of Qingshanli

1923

Colonial period
Bang Jeonghwan
establishes Children's Day

1923

Colonial period
Kanto Massacre takes
place in Japan

Righteous armies had existed since before the Protectorate Treaty. You may remember the important events of 1895, when Empress Myeongseong was assassinated by the Japanese and the top-knot edict was issued. That year saw numerous righteous uprisings.

The first righteous armies were led by Confucian scholars, who were even more outraged by the top-knot edict than by the slaying of the empress. Their Neo-Confucian educations had taught them that no part of the bodies they had inherited from their parents, not even a single strand of hair, should be damaged. Cutting off top-knots would mean reducing themselves to barbarians, they argued, so they formed righteous armies to punish the Japanese and their Korean stooges.

'Expel evil and uphold propriety'
This was the slogan branded by Confucian scholars leading righteous armies: "propriety" meant Neo-Confucianism, while "evil" was a reference to Western culture.

But righteous armies really came into their own after the Daehan imperial army was disbanded. Remember how Japan ordered its dissolution in 1907? Many former imperial soldiers now joined righteous armies, strengthening them almost beyond recognition thanks to their professional military training.

A united righteous army alliance advances on Seoul

In December 1907, well-known *yangban* righteous army commanders such as Yi Inyeong, Yi Gangnyeon and Heo Wi formed an alliance that they named the Righteous Army of the Thirteen Provinces.

Some 10,000 righteous army soldiers from across Joseon met at Yangju in Gyeonggi-do Province, not far from the capital. There, they held a conference and chose Yi Inyeong and Heo Wi, respectively, as their commander-in-chief and head of operations. Soon the alliance was fully prepared: all that remained was to advance on Seoul. Just then, Yi Inyeong received news that his father had died. "Disloyalty to my country means failing to perform my duty as a son," he said, "and vice versa." In accordance with Neo-

Each region had righteous armies of its own. Yu Inseok led one in Chuncheon, Yi Gangnyeon one in Gyeongsang-do Province, and so on. Later, several armies came together to advance on Seoul and drive out the Japanese.

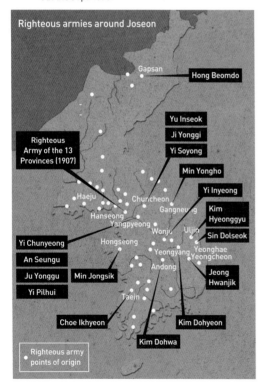

Righteous armies around Joseon

Gapsan
Hong Beomdo
Yu Inseok
Ji Yonggi
Yi Soyong
Min Yongho
Righteous Army of the 13 Provinces (1907)
Yi Inyeong
Haeju
Chuncheon
Kim Hyeonggyu
Hanseong
Gangneung
Yangpyeong
Sin Dolseok
Wonju
Uljin
Yi Chunyeong
Hongseong
Yeongyang
Yeonghae
An Seungu
Yeongcheon
Ju Yonggu
Min Jongsik
Andong
Jeong Hwanjik
Yi Pilhui
Taein
Choe Ikhyeon
Kim Dohyeon
Kim Dohwa
Righteous army points of origin

Confucian custom, he abandoned all his other duties and returned to his home to mourn his father for three years. Heo Wi took his place as leader of the alliance.

Under Heo's command, the Righteous Army of the Thirteen Provinces advanced to within thirty *ri* of Seoul, where it was defeated by Japanese forces. The carefully planned offensive to take the capital had ended in failure. By the way, what do you think about Yi Inyeong's decision to abandon his troops just before their most important battle in order to mourn his father? Would you have done the same?

The ranks of the righteous armies included peasants, hunters, farmhands and professional soldiers. The poor farmers fought hardest of all. A large number of former

Righteous soldiers
Farmers, soldiers from the disbanded Daehan military and even young teenagers joined righteous armies. Despite their diverse backgrounds, their aims were the same.

Arrested righteous army leaders
Righteous armies were led by *yangban* but consisted largely of commoners. They all sought to defend their country.

Donghak revolutionaries joined the righteous armies in opposition to interference by Japan and Western powers, attacking Japanese landowners and their stooges.

Japan felt the need to neutralize the righteous armies, which were fighting with ever more ferocity as time passed. It launched a crackdown in the southern part of the peninsula, laying waste to Jeolla-do Province and hunting down righteous army fighters throughout Gangwon-do and Hwanghae-do. Lasting around two months, the operation saw some 100 righteous army commanders and 4,000 troops captured or killed. It was now almost impossible for the rebels to operate within Joseon, and those that remained crossed the Dumangang and Amnokgang rivers into Chinese Manchuria or Russia's Primorsky Krai province. There, they continued their anti-Japanese struggle in the guise of independence fighters.

Sin Dolseok, the 'Tiger of Mt. Taebaeksan'

As I've just mentioned, most righteous army commanders were initially *yangban*, who gathered and led commoner troops. As time passed, however, commanders of commoner origin also appeared.

Choe Ikhyeon - 'yangban' and righteous army commander

"You can cut off my head, but never my hair!"

Choe Ik-hyeon was outraged by the top-knot edict, which ordered all men in the Daehan Empire to cut off their top-knots. The *yangban* righteous army commander was famous for his integrity and pride. In 1906, the year after the signing of the Protectorate Treaty, he formed an army in Jeolla-do Province at the age of seventy-four. He was aided by Im Byeongchan, his disciple, but the pair were soon arrested and banished to the Japanese island of Tsushima.

In exile, Choe began a hunger strike in protest at the insolent attitude of a Japanese official. Three days later, after receiving an apology from the official in question, he began eating again. A few months after that, he died. Though Choe is commonly believed to have died of starvation while on hunger strike, *Daemado ilgi* ("Tsushima Diary"), a work by Im, records in detail that his hunger strike lasted for six meals, that he subsequently returned to eating, and that the actual cause of his death was an illness described as *pungjeung* (風症; something akin to a stroke).

Choe Ikhyeon
Choe formed a righteous army at the age of seventy-four but was arrested and taken to Tsushima, where he died. This portrait of him is by late-Joseon artist Chae Yongsin.

Birthplace of Sin Dolseok
Sin's original home no longer stands; this reproduction is based on surviving accounts of it. It is located in Yeongdeok-gun County, Gyeongsangbuk-do Province.

Leading *yangban* commanders included Yu Inseok, Choe Ikhyeon, Heo Wi, Yi Inyeong, Yi Gangnyeon and Yi Soeung, while their counterparts from the ranks of commoners were figures such as Sin Dolseok, known as the Tiger of Mt. Taebaeksan, hunter Hong Beomdo, farmhand "Andamsari" (An Gyuhong) and Jeon Haesan. Here, I'd like to tell you a little about the Tiger of Mt. Taebaksan.

Sin Dolseok was born into a peasant family in Yeonghae, Gyeongsangbuk-do Province. His actual first name was Taeho, while Dolseok was a name he acquired as a young boy. He is sometimes also referred to as Dolseon. They say his ancestors included *yangban*, but by the time Dolseok was born his family held the status of ordinary peasants. As a boy, he attended the *seodang* run by Yi Jungnip, a descendant of Toegye Yi Hwang, in the neighboring village, where he learned to read and write. Dolseok was thus sufficiently educated to write poetry in classical Chinese despite his low

Sin Dolseok's army in action
Here, Sin's men clash with Japanese forces in the Taebaek mountains. They held a number of secret bases there, from which they would launch raids both to the east and to the west, earning Sin a reputation for magical powers of self-transportation. This was an exceptionally brave army, of which the Japanese were terrified.
– Independence Hall of Korea

social status.

Sin became a righteous commander in 1906, at the age of twenty-nine, when he assembled an army in his home village of Bokdeomi. After first fighting with a righteous army at the age of nineteen, he had spent the next ten years galvanizing his resolve and was now able to gather a large following.

Many of Sin's subordinates were *yangban*, while several other aristocrats supported his army by providing money, food and shelter.

Sin and his men were warmly welcomed wherever they went, thanks to their consistent victories and the consideration they showed local villagers. Some 300 in number, they fought across a large swathe of the country. Sin built several secret bases in valleys deep within the Taebaek mountains, from which he crossed back and forth over the mountains into Gyeongsang-do Province, Gangwon-do Province and the east coast, ambushing Japanese troops. Sin's uncanny appearances in different places in rapid succession sparked rumors that he was using magic powers to transport himself. He and his men repeatedly flummoxed the Japanese army, which branded him the Tiger of Mt. Taebaeksan.

When the Righteous Army of the Thirteen Provinces advanced on Seoul, Sin was due to lead some 1,000 of his men as part of the alliance. For some reason, though, they dropped out on the way. Some say the Tiger was rejected by *yangban* righteous commanders on account of his commoner status; others say certain circumstances forced him and his men to withdraw. In any case, they fought hard in the Gyeongsang-do region, separately from the Righteous Army of the Thirteen Provinces.

The Japanese army went all-out to capture Sin's forces. As its suppressive efforts in Korea grew more intense, Sin considered moving to Manchuria. Just then, however, he met his end, murdered by a relative, Kim Sangnyeol, whom he was visiting, and Kim's younger brother. He was thirty-one years old.

One story holds that Kim and his brother, unable to resist the hefty price put on Sin's head by the Japanese, rendered him unconscious with drugged wine before beating him to death with a rock, cutting off his head and presenting it to Japanese troops. But the Japanese officer who received the head refused to pay the reward,

Sin Dolseok
This portrait of Sin was produced when a shrine was built to commemorate him in 1999. One of his descendants, who closely resembled him, posed as a model for the artist. According to his subordinates, Sin had a wide, pockmarked face, a swarthy complexion and a burly physique.

claiming that it had been offered only to those capturing Sin and bringing him in alive.

Sin's sudden death came as a shock to the people of Joseon. Despite his death, the memory of the Tiger of Mt. Taebaeksan lived on in their hearts and they continued to pass on legends of his exploits.

National self-improvement for independence

While many Koreans chose the path of armed resistance to Japan, others worked to educate the populace in the belief that higher standards of learning could save the country. Collectively, the campaigns conducted by these activists are known as the "patriotic enlightenment movement."

The patriotic enlightenment movement was the successor to the progressive faction that had instigated the Gapsin Coup in 1884 and the Independence Club, which had had Seoul's Independence Gate built in 1897. Its members believed that Korea had to become strong in order to defeat Japan; that greater popular ability was the key to national strength; and that developing education and industry was the path to greater ability. Many members of the patriotic enlightenment movement disapproved of the fierce fighting of the righteous armies, believing it a waste of innocent life and a reckless choice that damaged the country it was trying

Independence Club
This association held mass rallies called *Manmin Gongdonghoe* ("Joint Meetings of All the People"), free forums open to anybody for the free expression of opinion. These came as a breath of fresh air to the people of Joseon, who had not previously enjoyed such opportunities. But Gojong had the club disbanded after being startled by rumors that it planned to abolish the monarchy and have a president elected.

Patriotic books
Many books were written with the aim of instilling patriotism. They contained knowledge about Korean history, language, geography and philosophy.
– Independence Hall of Korea

Graduation ceremony at Osan School
This photo shows the second batch of graduates from Osan School, which was founded by businessman Yi Seunghun after a speech by An Changho inspired him to save his country by educating its people. The school was located in Jeongju, Pyeonganbuk-do Province, Yi's hometown.

to help.

The movement aimed to educate the Korean people by opening schools for children and youths and publishing a variety of newspapers, magazines and books. Its members stoked interest in national heritage and nationhood by studying Korean language and history. Schools appeared across the country, accompanied by the slogan "knowledge is power." Among the many new places of learning that sprang up were Daeseong School, founded by An Changho in Pyeongyang, and Osan School, opened by Yi Seunghun in Pyeonganbuk-do Province. Japan obstructed the patriotic enlightenment movement by closing schools established by Koreans, or only allowing them to be opened with the permission of the Government-General.

Enlightenment activists also published plenty of newspapers and magazines. The *Daehan maeil sinbo* ("Korea Daily News"), in particular, was owned by Ernest Bethell, an Englishman, and therefore subject to less interference than other publications. The paper frequently ran articles critical of Japan, which regarded it with disgust and bought it at the time of the annexation, reducing it to a mere mouthpiece of the Government-General.

Korean newspapers were published overseas, too, such as the *Sinhan minbo* (New Korea) in America, and the *Haejo sinmun* (Mainstream) and *Daedong gongbo* ("Korea Gazette") in Primorsky Krai.

Interest in Korean language and history increased greatly, too. Hangeul scholar Ju Sigyeong traveled around the country teaching Korean grammar at schools and night study sessions. Carrying a big sack of books wherever he went, he earned himself nicknames such as "Ju the Bundle." Ju contributed greatly to the development of Korea's native script, publishing various language books including *Gugeo munjeon eumhak* ("Phonetics of the Korean Language") and *Gugeo munbeop* ("Korean Grammar").

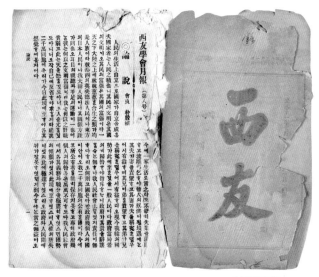

Newspapers and magazines that spearheaded the patriotic enlightenment movement
These publications appeared at the height of the patriotic enlightenment movement. At the top is a copy of *Seou* ("Western Friends") magazine; below are the *Jeguk sinmun* ("Imperial Post") on the left and the *Haejo sinmun* (Mainstream) on the right.
– Independence Hall of Korea

Ju Sigyeong
Ju became aware of the need for a unified system of Hangeul spelling while working at newspapers such as *The Independent* and the *Jeguk sinmun*. He then devoted his life to studying the Korean language.

Uniting to repay national debt

In early 1907, at the height of the patriotic enlightenment movement, an eye-catching article appeared in the *Daehan maeil sinbo*. It was jointly written by Kim Gwangje, the head of a Daegu-based publisher called Gwangmunsa, and his friend Seo Sangdon.

"Joseon owes Japan a debt of 13 million won," the article claimed. "If we want to escape Japanese rule, we must first repay it. So let's stop smoking for three months and gather 20 *jeon* from each of Joseon's 20 million people."

Joseon's population at the time was 20 million; the article called on all citizens to unite in order to pay off the national debt. Known as the "national debt redemption movement,"

Memorial to the women of the national debt redemption movement
Women contributed greatly to the the national debt redemption movement. The women's association in Namil-dong, Daegu, played a leading role by donating rings and silver knives. This stele in the shape of a traditional *garakji* ring was erected in a memorial park in Daegu to mark the centenary of the movement.

the proposal met with a hugely positive response as soon as the article was published.

Men stopped smoking, while women raised money by selling rings and jewelry. Women gave up their most precious rings and *norigae* (traditional accessories), schoolgirls shyly handed over money they had made by embroidering patterns through the night and selling them the next day—even *gisaeng* (courtesans), the objects of social contempt, gave generously out of a sense of civic duty...

But the national debt redemption movement, too, was ended by Japanese suppression. Yang Gitak, manager of the *Daehan maeil sinbo*, was arrested on trumped up charges of embezzlement, an event that deprived the movement of its momentum. The final blow came with Joseon's official annexation by Japan. So what happened to all the money raised in the mean time? Choe Eunhui, a journalist with the *Chosun ilbo* during the colonial period, claimed that she had heard that the Government-General had seized the funds, but that this was not certain.

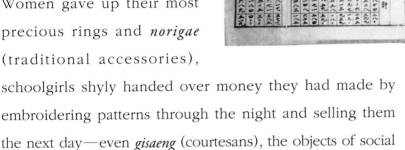

Record of funds collected for national debt redemption
Once the national debt redemption movement gathered momentum, the Japanese police began investigating how much money had been collected. This movement was similar to the gold-collecting campaign that took place during the financial crisis of 1998. At that time, too, Koreans showed a genuine sense of national unity by donating their most precious gold objects. But whereas those in 1998 were paid in cash for their gold, people donating to the earlier national debt redemption movement received nothing in return.
–Independence Hall of Korea

Yun Huisun and the Ansaram Righteous Army

Korean history is full of instances of strong women emerging at times of national crisis. Many took up arms and gave their lives fighting with the righteous armies, too. Yun Huisun and the Ansaram Righteous Army were a leading example. The word "*ansaram*" means "wife" or "woman."

Yun, leader of the Ansaram Righteous Army, was the eldest daughter-in-law of Yu Hongseok, having married Yun's eldest son at the age of sixteen. Yu Hongseok, meanwhile, was a cousin of Yu Inseok, a famous righteous army commander from Chuncheon.

Yun decided to join the fight against the Japanese as soon as her father-in-law formed a righteous army. When he tried to dissuade her, telling her the battlefield was no place for a woman, Yun secretly gathered women from the Yu household and the village. She wrote a song called *Ansaram uibyeong ga* ("Song of the Righteous Wives") and taught it to her fighters.

Eventually, Yun and her righteous army of some thirty women received the same military training as male righteous soldiers. They went around collecting funds for military campaigns, cooked and did laundry for other soldiers, and mixed cow dung and clay to make gunpowder for the righteous army's guns.

After the annexation, Yun and her family went to China. There, her father-in-law and husband died, but Yun remained undeterred. She devoted herself to publicizing *Ansaram uibyeong ga* ("Song of the Righteous Wives") and other anti-Japanese songs she had composed, gathered Korean comrades and took care of other righteous army fighters. Yun eventually died twelve days after her son, Donsang, lost his life in the fight for independence.

Ansaram uibyeong ga ("Song of the Righteous Wives")

No matter how strong the Nips may be
United, we'll beat them easily.
We may be women, but our patriotism is as strong as ever.
Man or woman, we're nothing without our country.
Let us join the righteous struggle!
We'd rather be ripped apart by wild beasts than serve the Japs.
Let us help the righteous armies!
Let us help the righteous armies!
If our country wins, it will last forever.
Long live the Ansaram Righteous Army!

Yun Huisun
Yun's remains were returned to South Korea in 1994, sixty years after her death. She left an autobiography titled Haeju Yun-ssi *ilsaengnok* ("A Record of the Life of Ms. Yun of Haeju").

CHAPTER 3

Gunfire echoes across Manchuria

Everything had happened in a flash. Just then, a booming voice emerged from somewhere behind the Russian troops:

"Korea *ura*! Korea *ura*!"

Ura means "long live" in Russian; the man shouting it was An Junggeun.

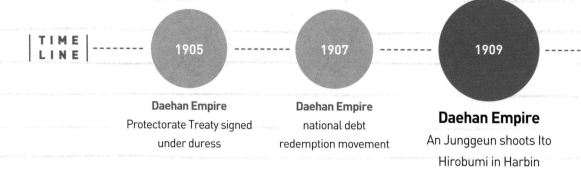

TIME
LINE

1905

Daehan Empire
Protectorate Treaty signed
under duress

1907

Daehan Empire
national debt
redemption movement

1909

Daehan Empire
An Junggeun shoots Ito
Hirobumi in Harbin

Have you seen the Korean film 2009: Lost Memories? *It's a fascinating story that speculates about what might have happened if An Junggeun hadn't assassinated Ito Hirobumi in Harbin. Ito, as you know, was the man who forced the Daehan Empire to sign the Protectorate Treaty that took away control of its foreign affairs.*

So what actually would have happened if An hadn't killed Ito? Perhaps the Republic of Korea wouldn't even exist, and the people that lived there now would have Japanese names like "Yoshiko" and "Shinichiro."

Scholars like to point out that there are no ifs in history. They mean that each event and incident happened for a reason that made it inevitable; that there are no coincidences. This concept is known as historical inevitability. Still, I do like to wander down the impossible pathways of if from time to time. It's a good way of realizing how important inevitability really is.

Today, let's go back to the October morning when An Junggeun assassinated Ito Hirobumi and find out just what made this incident another inevitable part of history.

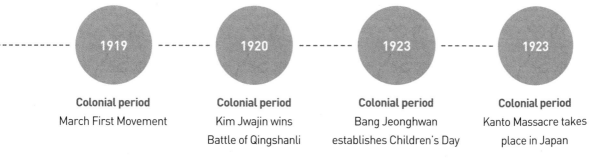

1919	1920	1923	1923
Colonial period	Colonial period	Colonial period	Colonial period
March First Movement	Kim Jwajin wins Battle of Qingshanli	Bang Jeonghwan establishes Children's Day	Kanto Massacre takes place in Japan

Four years had passed since the signing of the Protectorate Treaty. Japan was growing more powerful by the day, while Joseon was doing everything it could to save itself. An made his plan against this background.

It was nine o'clock in the morning on October 26, 1909, at Harbin Station in Manchuria. A train pulled slowly in. When it stopped, a short, bearded figure stepped down onto the platform: Ito Hirobumi. He had made his way to Harbin for a meeting with Russian finance minister Vladimir Kokovtsov, as the city was part of Russian territory at the time.

Harbin
Harbin is Manchuria's most important city. In the early twentieth century, it was of vital strategic importance as the hub of the region's growing transport network. Ito was to meet Kokovtsov here to discuss who would operate the railways in Manchuria. Another purpose of the meeting was to inform Russia of Japan's planned annexation of Joseon.

Ito Hirobumi in Harbin
Ito is the short figure with a white beard, located second from the left in this photo.

An shoots Ito

Russian soldiers waited in formation at Harbin Station to receive Ito. They were joined by local Japanese, who had turned up to welcome the visiting statesman. When Ito had inspected the Russian troops, he began greeting the well-wishers who had turned up to see him. Suddenly, three gunshots rang out.

Ito, making his way among the crowd, staggered backwards. Another three shots were fired. This time, three Japanese officials behind Ito fell to the ground in succession. Everything had happened in a flash. Just then, a booming voice emerged from somewhere behind the Russian troops:

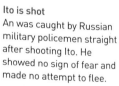

Ito is shot
An was caught by Russian military policemen straight after shooting Ito. He showed no sign of fear and made no attempt to flee.

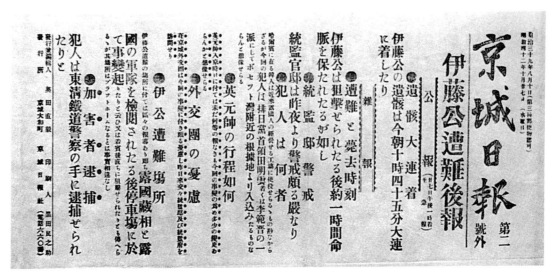

京城日報

伊藤公遭難後報

第二

號外

發行美國新聞人　奧田直毅　京城大和町京城日報社　印刷人　黒田民之助　（電話六六〇番）

犯人は東清鐵道警察の手に逮捕せられたりと

●加害者逮捕

伊公遭難場所に付ては諸々の報告されども未だ何等の要領を得日来交々交渉及び統監府を

●伊公遭難場所

英元帥の一行に付ては未だ何等の邪報の為め北少の搜索あらんとの報傳あり

●英元帥の行程如何

哈爾賓に在る韓人に乾參密謀の経営せらるゝものを知らざるが今回の犯人は排日黨首領田雷の根據地より入込みたるものな

犯人は何者

統監官邸は昨夜より警戒頗る嚴なり

●統監邸警戒

伊藤公は狙撃せられたるが脈を保たれたるが如し

遭難と薨去時刻

●遭難大連着

伊藤公の遺骸は今朝十時四十五分大連に着したり

遭難報

"Korea *ura*! Korea *ura*!"

Ura means "long live" in Russian; the man shouting it was An Junggeun. He was captured on the spot, while Ito was put back on the train, blood gushing from the three bullet holes in his body.

"I've been hit," Ito murmured. About thirty minutes later, at ten o'clock, he died.

After his arrest, An was held in a prison in Lüshun in Manchuria. He was tried at the High Court of Kwantung Leased Territory, along with fellow conspirators U Deoksun, Jo Doseon and Yu Dongha. The trial was heavily weighted against An, with a Japanese judge and Japanese prosecutors and lawyers. But he remained unafraid, confidently stating his position to the court:

"I killed Ito Hirobumi in my capacity as a righteous army officer, not as an assassin. Ito was the main culprit in

Newspaper report of Ito's assassination
This article in the *Gyeongseong ilbo* ("Gyeongseong Times") reports that An has been arrested. When asked why he killed Ito, An gave a list of fifteen answers. First, Ito had masterminded the assassination of Empress Myeongseong; second, he had forced the Daehan emperor to abdicate; third, he had forced the Protectorate Treaty on the Daehan Empire; and so on.

damaging relations between Joseon and Japan and disturbing the peace in East Asia. My elimination of him therefore constituted a military operation. Consequently, I am here as a prisoner of war, captured in battle, and I hope that you will punish me in accordance with international law."

A lieutenant general in the righteous army

An labelled himself a righteous soldier. But today, many are unaware of his active service in the righteous army despite his fame as Ito's killer. Here is the story of An's military career.

An was born in 1879 in Haeju, Hwanghae-do Province, the eldest son of a *yangban* family. He was an impetuous boy by nature, so his father gave him a name that might convey the kind of gravitas he hoped would temper his son's behavior. *Jung* (重) means "heavy," while *geun* (根) means "root" and can also mean "mind." Like all *yangban* boys, An had to study Confucianism. But he much preferred putting his books aside and taking a gun into the mountains to hunt. He was an excellent marksman, renowned locally for his shooting skills.

When he was sixteen, An married Kim Aryeo. The couple had two sons and a daughter. Around this time, he became a Catholic, was baptized by a French priest and received the baptismal name Thomas. He learned

An Junggeun
This image was taken at a prison in Lüshun in 1909 after An assassinated Ito.

French and studied Western culture.

The Protectorate Treaty prompted An to join the struggle to save Joseon. Angered at his country's loss of diplomatic control, he founded a school in the

An and his comrades
This image shows An in court with U Deoksun, Jo Doseon and Yu Dongha, the comrades that helped him plan Ito's assassination. An, seen here in the front row on the far right, was sentenced to death, U to three years in prison and Jo and Yu to eighteen months each.

belief that what Joseon needed most urgently was talented, well-educated individuals. The patriotic Korean devoted himself to education, serving as principal of Donui and Samheung schools, the respective equivalents of a modern elementary and middle school.

Around this time, Gojong was forced to abdicate as a result of the secret mission he sent to the Hague and the Daehan imperial army was disbanded. An now decided that education was no longer enough to save his country and began looking for other means. Certain that Japan would declare war in the future, he decided it was necessary to form a righteous army and fight the enemy directly. To this end, he traveled to Vladivostok, a city with a large Korean population. Once in Russia, An made his way around local villages giving speeches aimed at recruiting righteous fighters.

"Things go wrong when people give up hope that they themselves can bring about change. In other words, things go right when we decide we can change them. That's why they say, 'Heaven helps those who help themselves.' So I ask you: What is right? Sitting back and waiting for death to come to us, or taking responsibility and acting for ourselves?"

An's powerful speeches made a deep impression on those who heard them. Soon, he had gathered 300 Koreans ready to train. An became a lieutenant general in his unit; Kim Duseong was commander in chief and Yi Beomyun governor. An's unit remained in contact with that of Hong Beomdo, one of the best-known righteous armies of the time, planning attacks on Japanese troops in the Hamgyeong-do region.

The Finger Cutting League

An's unit crossed the Dumangang River into Hamgyeongbuk-do Province, where it fought against and defeated Japanese troops at Gyeongheung. The unit took several Japanese prisoners of war, but An set them all free in accordance with international law:

"No part of international law calls for the killing of captured enemy troops," he said. "You keep them prisoner, then send them home later on in exchange for compensation."

Highly commendable though they were, An's actions brought bad results. Others began to disapprove of him,

An's handprint
An signed this piece of calligraphy "An Junggeun of Korea," followed by his handprint. He wrote it while in prison in Lüshun. Notice how the ring finger of his left hand is unusually short: this is because An cut it off above the top knuckle while swearing an oath of loyalty to the Finger Cutting League. He was an excellent calligrapher and often wrote short texts like this for those who knew him in prison, including the Japanese guards.

finding his releasing of Japanese prisoners preposterous. Worse still, the soldiers he had released promptly gave away the location of his unit, which was then defeated in a surprise attack by the Japanese. Its surviving members scattered and An, barely managing to escape with his life, returned to Vladivostok. Despite the cool reception he now received, he refused to give up hope.

Have you ever seen An's left handprint? The ring finger is strangely short: this is because An was a member of the so-called "Finger Cutting League."

In January 1909, An Junggeun and eleven of his comrades cut off the top segments of their left-hand ring fingers, wrote "Daehan Independence" in their own blood on a Taegeukgi (Korean flag) and swore to dedicate themselves to their country. Soon after forming the Finger Cutting League, An learned that Ito was on his way to Manchuria and decided to take action.

Just as he claimed, it was as a righteous soldier in battle that An killed Ito. In court, he claimed that he should be released as a prisoner of war, just as he had earlier set his

Postcard commemorating the Finger Cutting League
This postcard was produced in tribute to An and his eleven comrades in the league.
– Independence Hall of Korea

An speaks his last words
Two days before his execution, An met his two younger brothers and Catholic priest Hong Seok-gu to deliver his final words. He vowed to continue working for his country even after he died. Father Hong was a Frenchman who had baptized An.

own Japanese prisoners of war free. Unfortunately, he was accorded no such treatment.

A 'righteous war' for peace in East Asia

In prison, An wrote his autobiography and gave it the title *An Eungchil yeoksa* ("The History of An Eungchil"). Eungchil had been An's childhood name: it implied that the seven spots on his belly and chest meant he had been born with the cosmic energy of the Big Dipper.

An's autobiography covered everything from his birth to his assassination of Ito, including his righteous army campaigns. He also recorded his frustration at being tried in a court full of Japanese people:

"I'm not sure if what's happening to me is real or just a dream. I'm as Korean as they come, so why am I in a

'An Eungchil yeoksa'
An wrote this autobiography while in prison. "On July 16 of 1879, the year *eulmyo,* a boy was born below Mt. Suyangsan in Haejubu, Hwanghae-do Province, Daehan..." the book begins, going on to provide a frank account of its author's life.

White on yellow
When the Russo-Japanese War broke out, it was seen by many as a struggle between white and yellow races, and between the West and the East. For this reason, a number of Koreans supported Japan, even though it was on the verge of taking over their country. An was one of them. This cartoon satirizing the conflict appeared in a French newspaper. Russia is portrayed as the giant "European champion," standing on Manchuria while Japan, the little "Asian champion" stands with one foot on Japan and the other on the Korean Peninsula.

Japanese prison? And why am I being tried according to Japanese laws? When did I become a Japanese citizen? The judge is Japanese, as are the lawyers, the prosecutors, the interpreter and the spectators. It's as if the deaf have turned up to listen to speeches from the dumb. Is this some kind of dream world? If so, it's about time to wake up."

After completing his autobiography, An began work on a book called *Dongyang pyeonghwaron* ("On Peace in East Asia"). It remained unfinished, however, as An was executed after writing just the foreword and part of the first chapter.

The empty tomb of An Junggeun Of these four tombs, the one on the left, without a tombstone, belongs to An. It is currently empty. Nobody yet knows what was done with his remains; the empty tomb was built in the hope that they will be located and returned one day. Surely today's Koreans and their descendants should make an effort to find An and bring him home? The tombs are in Seoul's Hyochang Park.

Nonetheless, *Dongyang pyeonghwaron* contains a synthesis of An's thoughts. Let's look at this passage, which should give us some idea of why An killed Ito:

"It doesn't take a genius to work out that the best way to deal with the hardship caused by Western powers spreading into East Asia is for the countries here to unite and resist together. So why is Japan ignoring the situation and attacking its neighbor, another country of yellow people? Nothing is easier for a fisherman than when he comes across an oystercatcher and an oyster struggling with each other: he simply walks up and catches them both. Does Japan really want to be caught by a Western fisherman as it messes in the mud with Joseon?"

It will doubtless surprise you that many Koreans supported Japan during the Russo-Japanese War. They saw the conflict as a struggle between yellow and white races; between the aggressive West and the defiant East. Even leading patriotic newspapers such as *The Independent* and the *Capital Gazette* sometimes ran articles calling for unity between Qing, Joseon and Japan for the protection of East Asian culture and yellow races. Of course, Japan's own propaganda was partly responsible for spreading the notion that it was out to defend peace in the region.

An Junggeun, too, held a similar view of Japan at the time. But when it forced the Protectorate

Bronze statue of An
An was executed at around ten in the morning on March 26, 1910, in Lüshun Prison. He was thirty-two years old. This statue and stele stand on Mt. Namsan in Seoul.

Stele with a quotation from An
The inscription reads, in Chinese, "I am ever anxious about the safety of my country".

Treaty on Joseon after defeating Russia, An realized what it was really up to. Despite its loud calls for peace in East Asia,

Punishing the 'Five Eulsa Traitors'

The five ministers who agreed to the signing of the Protectorate Treaty—Yi Wanyong, Yi Jiyong, Park Jesun, Yi Geuntaek and Gwon Junghyeon—are known collectively as the Five Eulsa Traitors (*eulsa* being the calendar name of 1905). These men were the object of widespread anger for betraying their country. Na Cheol (an alias of Na Inyeong) made the first call for their punishment, forming a death squad with O Giho (an alias of O Hyeok) and plotting to kill them all.

Na Cheol and his comrades
These men formed a death squad to kill the Five Eulsa Traitors. Na stands in the back row on the left.

Members of the death squad waited in pre-appointed positions for their targets, but were unable to assassinate them when they passed by because of their tight Japanese military escorts. Still, the attempt itself was enough to scare the Five Eulsa Traitors out of their wits. And it was followed by a string of other incidents. American diplomat Durham Stevens, who supported Japan's moves towards colonizing Korea, was gunned down in San Francisco by expatriate Koreans Jeon Myeongun and Jang Inhwan, while Yi Wanyong was seriously injured in a knife attack by Yi Jaemyeong.

After his failed attempt to kill the Five Eulsa Traitors, Na Cheol founded a religion called Daejongism, based on the worship of Dangun. Despite persecution by the Japanese authorities, the new faith proved highly influential among independence activists.

Japan actually wanted to take over the entire region for itself. Once he was aware of this, An killed Ito, a leading proponent of the Protectorate Treaty, for the sake of genuine regional peace.

In *Dongyang pyeonghwaron*, An described his assassination of Ito as "a righteous war for peace in East Asia." Hopefully you now understand his reasons.

An's deed was not enough to stop Korea becoming a Japanese colony: the death of a single statesman was not enough to change the policies of a government. In the end, the Treaty of Annexation was signed around a year after An's death. Still, the assassination did serve to deliver the message to Japan, Joseon and the West that An's country was not prepared to simply roll over and die.

A learned man's burden

News of the annexation by Japan left many Koreans devastated. While some of them took up arms and fought, like An Junggeun, others protested by taking their own lives.

Hwang Hyeon was among those who chose suicide in his bitterness at the loss of Joseon's sovereignty. Before he died, he left four poems deeply infused with his love for his country. Here's one of them:

Hear the birds and beasts wail in sorrow; see the mountains and rivers convulse in grief.

The land of the Rose of Sharon is no more.

Closing my book in the autumn lamplight, I reflect on our history.

How hard it is to live a conscientious life!

After agonizing over the what an educated man should do when his country had been stripped of its own sovereignty, Hwang attempted to fulfill his duty by killing himself. What would you have done?

A native of Gwangyang in Jeolla-do Province, Hwang passed the state examination with the highest score in his year. But the political tumult of his times made him turn his back

Hwang Hyeon

Hwang wrote books including *Maecheon yarok* ("Unofficial Records from Maecheon") and *Oha gimun* ("News Recorded under the Paulownia Tree"), as well as numerous poems. *Maecheon yarok* records some fifty years from the beginning of Gojong's reign, in 1864, to the annexation in 1910, a hugely important time in Korean history, as witnessed first-hand by Hwang. The final part of the book, covering the period from August 29, 1910 to September 10 of the same year, when Hwang took his own life, was written by one of his disciples. This photo was taken in Cheonyeondang Studio in Seoul, when Hwang was fifty-five.

on a government career and devote himself to contemplating his country's future. His attitude contrasts sharply with that of men like Yi Wanyong, who were quite happy to occupy top government posts while approving the Protectorate Treaty and the Treaty of Annexation. Many others, including Min Yeonghwan and Yi Beomjin, also took their own lives in anguish at losing their country.

CHAPTER 4

The nation rises up

One of the students climbed onto the rostrum and began reading out the document:

"We hereby proclaim that Joseon is an independent country and that it belongs to its people. We declare to all the countries of the world that humankind is equal, and that our people shall enjoy in perpetuity the natural right to independent existence."

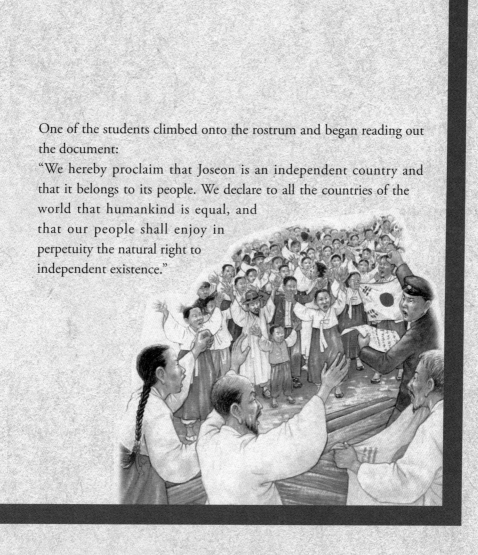

TIME LINE	1905	1907	1909
	Daehan Empire Protectorate Treaty signed under duress	**Daehan Empire** National Movement for Debt Redemption	**Daehan Empire** An Junggeun shoots Ito Hirobumi in Harbin

Have you ever wondered why the March First Movement happened on March 1?

In fact, the movement was triggered by Gojong's funeral. The former emperor died quite suddenly, giving rise to a series of rumors including that he had been poisoned by the Japanese or had killed himself in indignation after one of his sons, Eun, had married a Japanese princess. As the rumors multiplied, public antipathy towards Japan reached new heights.

March 3 was announced as the date of Gojong's funeral. Mourners from all over the country began pouring into the capital several days in advance, traveling by train or boat or walking through the night if necessary.

Gojong's death brought sorrow and anger at the loss of Korea's sovereignty to bursting point, ready to erupt at the slightest provocation. Can you imagine how the atmosphere have been?

Let's go back to early 1919 and see what was going on.

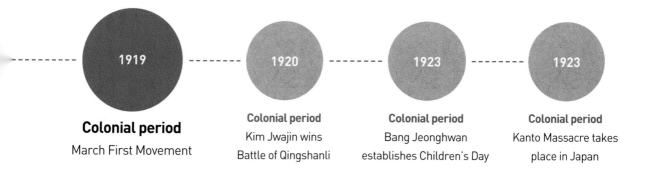

1919

Colonial period

March First Movement

1920

Colonial period

Kim Jwajin wins

Battle of Qingshanli

1923

Colonial period

Bang Jeonghwan

establishes Children's Day

1923

Colonial period

Kanto Massacre takes

place in Japan

Preparation for the March First Movement had long been underway. Cheondoist, Protestant and Buddhist leaders, together with students, took the lead in preparing plans for a nationwide independence campaign. When Gojong died, they decided to launch the movement to coincide with his funeral, when mourners from all over the country would be gathered in the capital. Avoiding the day of the actual funeral, they chose a date two days in advance: Saturday, March 1.

On the night of February 28, the leaders of the movement selected thirty-three representatives: fifteen Cheondoists including Son Byeonghui, Choe Rin, Gwon Dongjin and O Sechang; Buddhists Han Yongun and Baek Yongseong; and sixteen Protestants including Yi Seunghun, Gil Seonju, Yi

Gojong's funeral procession
Gojong died suddenly in January, 1919, prompting rumors that the Japanese had poisoned him. Though Joseon had lost its sovereignty by then, people traveled from all over the country to mourn their former emperor.

Choe Namseon's 'Declaration of Independence'
The text of Choe's declaration contains many Chinese characters, making it hard for young Koreans today to read. In 1919, too, it would only have made sense to those who were lucky enough to be educated. Though he wrote the declaration, Choe was not among the thirty-three popular representatives who issued it.
– Independence Hall of Korea

Gapseong and Park Huido. There were no Confucians among them.

Religious figures led the March First Movement because theirs were the only groups left by the colonial regime with any power to organize large numbers of people. Moreover, many other leading independence activists had fled overseas to avoid persecution. The representatives decided to print copies of an independence declaration drafted by Choe Namseon and deliver it from door to door.

The representatives gather at a restaurant

March 1, 1919 finally arrived. Copies of the declaration of independence were delivered and posters put up at Dongdaemun Gate, Namdaemun Gate and Sookmyung Girl's Common High School, announcing the start of the independence movement. By two in the afternoon, crowds had filled Tapgol Park and Jongno, the large street in front of it, waiting for the thirty-three representatives to appear.

The thirty-three representatives Son Byeonghui and the other popular representatives gathered at Taehwagwan, a restaurant near Tapgol Park. They had decided to issue the Declaration of Independence here, instead of at the park. Taehwagwan was owned by An Sunhwan, a former palace chef who had once prepared the king's meals. Today, a modern building stands in its place.

–Independence Hall of Korea

Tapgol Park
The March First Movement began at this park, on the northern side of central Seoul's Jongno 3-ga Street. A temple called Wongaksa, which had a ten-story pagoda, once stood here. In 1897, the site became Joseon's first Western-style park, named Tapgol Gongwon ("Pagoda Park"). The *tap* part of the park's present name means "tower" or "pagoda." On the left of this photo, in the distance, is a bronze statue of Son Byeonghui, one of the thirty-three popular representatives.

Meanwhile, twenty-nine of the representatives were gathered at Taehwagwan, a nearby restaurant, the remaining four having failed to make the journey from the provinces. Several students ran over from the park to find out what was keeping them.

"There's a big crowd waiting," they said. "Please come quickly!"

"We've decided to read out the declaration here," they replied. "It's the only way to avoid starting a riot."

The students pleaded with them not to change their plans at the last moment, but the representatives merely sent them back to the park and refused to budge. Instead, they read out the statement and held a round of cheers for independence in the restaurant. Now, the Japanese police turned up—they say it was the representatives themselves who had called them. Which means, if it's true, that the representatives turned themselves in. The police bundled them into five cars and whisked them away.

When the crowds eagerly awaiting the representatives at Tapgol Park heard the news, they decided to make the declaration themselves. It was now half-past two. One of the students climbed onto the rostrum and began reading out the document:

March First Demonstrations
This crowd at Tapgol Park stands electrified as a student reads out the Declaration of Independence. Ones he has finished, it begins cheering wildly.

Cheering demonstrators
This crowd outside Ginyeombijeon Pavilion, near Gwanghwamun Gate, had gathered to cheer for independence. People of all ages turned out, from young children with ribbons in their hair to old men in horsehair hats.

"We hereby proclaim that Joseon is an independent country and that it belongs to its people. We declare to all the countries of the world that humankind is equal, and that our people shall enjoy in perpetuity the natural right to independent existence."

The crowd stood in complete silence, absorbing every word. After some time, a chorus of cheers for independence broke out.

The united voices of the crowd filled the sky and shook the ground. With singing students in the lead, a procession began making its way through the streets of the capital. The students exhorted their 20 million fellow Koreans to rise up, take up arms and wrest back their homeland and freedom from the hands of the Japanese.

The cheering crowd grew steadily larger as visiting mourners from all over the country joined its ranks. It passed through Jongno Street, past Seoul Station, Jeong-dong, Gwanghwamun, and Seodaemun and Seosomun gates, growing all the while. Merchants hurriedly closed their shops and joined in, while women, children and the elderly all came out into the streets, cheering. Old ladies handing out water to the crowds ending up joining them, waving their dippers high in ecstasy. That day, the streets of Seoul echoed with cheers for independence.

Misplaced hope: the principle of self-determination

Why, then, did the thirty-three representatives choose to stay in the restaurant instead of showing up at Tapgol Park, as agreed? In fact, they had taken this decision at their final meeting the previous evening. "If we make the declaration

Korean students in Tokyo declare independence

The March First Movement was not the first time Koreans had attempted to declare independence from Japanese rule. It was preceded by the "Muo Independence Declaration," issued by thirty-nine activists in Manchuria in November, 1918 (*muo* being the calendar name for that year), and by the "February Eighth Declaration," made by Korean students in Japan in early 1919.

The Tokyo students' February declaration proved hugely inspiring to

Korean pro-independence students in Japan
Some 400 Korean students in Tokyo, including Choe Paryong, Seo Chun, Baek Gwansu, Yi Jonggeun and Song Gyebaek, gathered at a Korean Christian youth association in Tokyo to declare their country's independence.

activists in Joseon itself, prompting preparations for the March First Movement. Here's an excerpt:

"On behalf of our 20 million compatriots, we declare before the countries of the world where justice and freedom have triumphed that Joseon will achieve independence. ... We hereby proclaim that independence will be attained through the exercising of freedom for the sake of our nation."

The principle of national self-determination
This principle was invoked at the end of World War I by victorious powers America, Britain and France in order to grant independence to the colonies of defeated Germany. Their aim was to stop their enemy from ever becoming so powerful again.

in a crowded place, people will go wild and it will lead to violence," they reasoned.

This may sound plausible enough, but what the representatives actually believed was that nationwide popular protests would not lead to independence. They lacked confidence in the power of the people, thinking instead that independence could only be won through diplomatic appeals for help from the great powers.

This belief was strongly influenced by then-US president Woodrow Wilson's emphasis on the principle of national self-determination. News that Germany's former colonies had been granted independence based on this principle filled Joseon's independence activists with hope. Surely the doctrine would apply to their country, too?

Their hope, however, proved misplaced. The principle of self-determination was applied only to the colonies of powers like Germany, Austro-Hungary and the Ottoman Empire after their defeat in World War I. The victors—the United States, Britain and France—were on good terms with Japan at this time, and had no intention of applying the principle to its colonies. No matter how hard Joseon pleaded for independence, then, the great powers failed to bat an eyelid.

But Joseon's popular leaders, lacking a firm grasp of the international situation, remained unilaterally enamored with the Western powers they believed would come to their rescue. How different might things have been if they had believed in their own people, with their burning desire for independence? I ask myself this every time I think of the thirty-three representatives.

The floodgates burst

The independence movement soon spread from Seoul to the rest of the country. Though its name, the March First Movement, suggests that all events were confined to a single day, this was not the case. In fact, the campaign kept going in various parts of the country for a whole year. Cheers for independence rang out everywhere from the biggest cities to the smallest villages, which should give you some idea of how desperately the people of Joseon longed to be free.

Though the initial movement was spearheaded by students, farmers, laborers and merchants all came to play leading roles as time went by. Patriotism knew no bounds when it came to age, sex or social status. On Jeju-do Island, the movement was led by women and children. Here's one of the most popular independence songs from back then:

Korean delegates at Paris Peace Conference
Korean independence activists in China sent delegates to Paris Peace Conference to let the world know that Japan had colonized Korea. In the front row on the left is Kim Gyusik, one of the delegates.

Finally, the voice of Joseon independence rings out,

After ten long years suppressed!

New life flows throughout the land and its 20 million people,

as we cheer together for a free, independent nation!

Japan was ruthless in its persecution of those who joined the movement. Its policemen, on horseback and armed with hammers and clubs, rounded up any cheering activists they came across. At the village of Jeam-ri in Suwon, they locked the villagers in a church and set fire to it, shooting anyone who managed to escape the blaze. Several dozen people lost their lives in Jeam-ri; similar incidents took place throughout the country.

Nobody knows exactly how many people were killed or injured. But statistics covering two months between March and May allow us to at least guess at the total. During this period, around 1,500 independence demonstrations took place, with some 2 million participants. Approximately 7,500 of them died, 15,000 were injured and 46,000 arrested. Given that the movement actually went on for a whole year, this should give you some idea of what the total figures may have been. Among

Independence demonstration in America
The March First Movement in Korea was followed by independence demonstrations in several other countries. This photo shows Koreans in the US holding a protest to demand their nation's sovereignty back.

Jeam-ri March First Movement Martyrdom Hall
The village of Jeam-ri was burned to the ground by Japanese troops. This photo shows the memorial hall built to mark the event.

the casualties was Yu Gwansun, well-known today as the Ewha Hakdang (now Ewha Girls' High School) student who was arrested for playing a leading role in an independence demonstration and tortured to death. Countless other nameless individuals shared Yu's fate at this time.

Despite the loss of many lives, the March First Movement eventually ended without achieving its goal. It had simply lacked the strength to carry on in the face of such harsh oppression. Should we regard it as a failure, then? Not necessarily. Though it didn't bring independence for Joseon, it did signal a new beginning for the country's independence fighters.

Those who joined the protests had undergone a

Yu Gwansun at Ewha Hakdang
Yu, a student at Ewha Hakdang, was arrested after traveling to Cheonan, her hometown, to take part in an independence demonstration. She died after being taken to Seoul's Seodaemun Prison and tortured. Here, Yu stands in the back row on the far right.
– Independence Hall of Korea

School record noting independence activism
This is the school record of Jo Gyeongmin, a student at Sookmyung Girls' High School. It states that, on March 5, 1919, she sneaked out of her dormitory and took part in the independence demonstrations.
– Sookmyung girl's high school

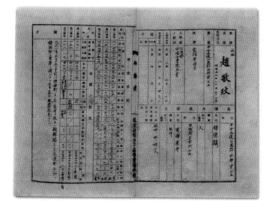

transformation. No one who had cheered for independence among the pulsing crowds could forget the overwhelming emotion and sense of liberation it brought. While independence movements had previously been regarded as the preserve of scholars or the leisured classes, they now seemed possible, even obligatory, for farmers, workers and everyone else. The March First Movement had propelled everyday Koreans to the forefront of the struggle—surely that, in itself, was enough to make it a success?

The movement also brought an awareness that the independence struggle demanded more thorough preparation and diverse action. Those who realized this now made their way out of Joseon into Chinese Manchuria and Russia's Primorsky Krai and went about their mission with renewed

determination. They formed a provisional government, believing such a centralized organ to be vital for the independence movement.

The Provisional Government of the Republic of Korea based itself in Shanghai and began using the name Daehan Minguk, instead of Joseon, to refer to Korea. (The former is the official name still used today by the Republic of Korea.) The country was now represented by its own government, albeit a provisional one.

Office of the Shanghai Provisional Government
This building was used by the Provisional Government of the Republic of Korea. After the March First Movement, campaigns to establish a provisional government began in Shanghai, the Soviet Union and Seoul itself. All independence activists, in Joseon and overseas, felt the need for such a government to lead their activities. After discussions, the three provisional governments united and were based in Shanghai.

'Gisaeng' fight for independence

One day in Haeju, Hwanghae-do Province, an unusual scene unfolded. Five women, dressed in white clothes and Taegeukgi bandanas, led a march for independence, cheering and waving flags.

The Japanese police soon showed up and arrested them, but the women carried on cheering even as they were taken away, throwing stones and breaking the windows and the police station. The five were local *gisaeng*, and their names were Kim Wolhui, Mun Wolseon, Kim Haejungwol, Mun Hyanghui and Ok Chaeju.

Kim Wolhui had experienced the March First Movement while in Seoul for Gojong's funeral. Emphatic that *gisaeng* were no different from other citizens, she decided to play her part in the independence struggle. Kim gathered fellow *gisaeng*, bit her finger until it bled, and painted a Taegeukgi in her own blood. They then began demonstrating. The Japanese police, convinced that *gisaeng* were incapable of protesting on their own initiative, tortured them to find out who had put them up to their act. But the women refused to be broken, even when they were covered in bruises and festering scars from being burned and whipped.

"We're different from Japanese geisha," they said. "We know how to love our own country."

Gisaeng demonstrated in Jinju, Tongyeong, and Suwon, too. In Jinju, thirty-two of them, led by Park Geumhyang, came together, waving flags and cheering. Invoking the Japanese invasions of the late sixteenth century, they called for their colonial occupiers to leave the country.

Most *gisaeng* came from poor families and had been sold into their profession. Those who know the meaning of real pain tend to understand the suffering of others and the value of community. It seems natural that *gisaeng*, with their harsh experiences of poverty and the sorrow of being despised by society, stood up and fought so resolutely for independence.

Women demand liberation
Korean history is full of examples of women stepping forward in times of national crisis, setting an example for their descendants today. These women are holding a pro-independence demonstration as part of the March First Movement.

CHAPTER 5

Hong Beomdo and Kim Jwajin, independence army heroes

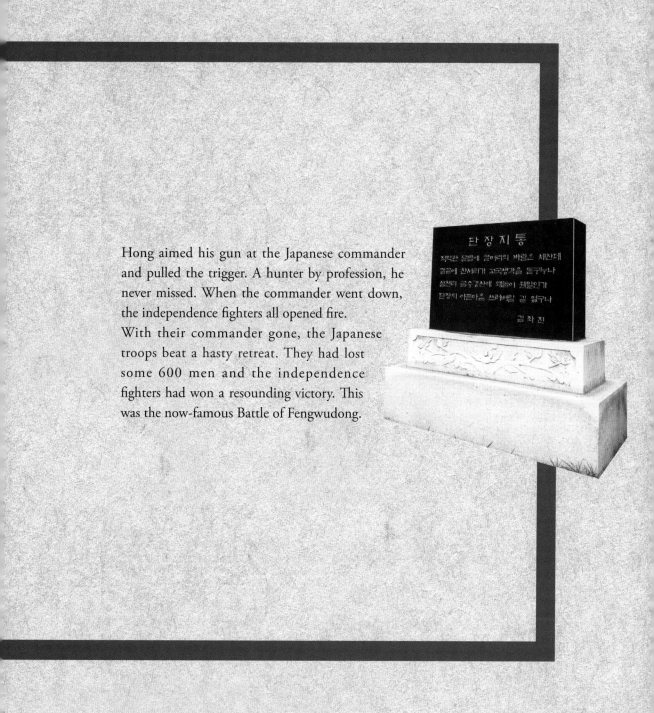

Hong aimed his gun at the Japanese commander and pulled the trigger. A hunter by profession, he never missed. When the commander went down, the independence fighters all opened fire.
With their commander gone, the Japanese troops beat a hasty retreat. They had lost some 600 men and the independence fighters had won a resounding victory. This was the now-famous Battle of Fengwudong.

단 장 지 통

적막한 달밤에 굴머리의 바람은 세찬데
굴풀에 찬서리가 고국생각을 돋구누나
삼천리 금수강산에 왜놈이 웬말인가
단장의 아픈마음 쓰러버릴 길 없도구나

김 좌 진

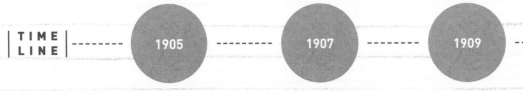

TIME LINE	1905	1907	1909
	Daehan Empire	**Daehan Empire**	**Daehan Empire**
	Protectorate Treaty signed under duress	national debt redemption movement	An Junggeun shoots Ito Hirobumi in Harbin

Have you ever seen a Korean TV drama depicting the independence hero Kim Jwajin? If so, you may wonder whether he really was as great as he's made out to be. In fact, he was. Kim led independence fighters against the Japanese during the colonial period, taking up arms to fight for his country's freedom.

Does that mean he was part of a righteous army, like An Junggeun? After the annexation of Joseon by Japan, the country's righteous soldiers moved into areas of Manchuria, Siberia and Primorsky Krai. They built new bases, formed bigger units and continued the fight against Japan. These forces are generally known as "independence armies."

Why did the independence armies operate from outside Joseon? Because the whole country was under Japanese control and building bases on Korean soil was impossible. Manchuria, Siberia and maritime Russia were closest to the border, allowing the independence armies to terrify the colonial authorities by crossing into Joseon for frequent raids and ambushes. Let's see what they got up to.

1919
Colonial period
March First
Movement

1920
Colonial period
Kim Jwajin wins Battle
of Qingshanli

1923
Colonial period
Bang Jeonghwan
establishes Children's Day

1923
Colonial period
Kanto Massacre takes
place in Japan

Rather than a unified army, Joseon's independence fighters organized themselves into various smaller units, each with its own name: the Korean Independence Army, the Northern Route Military Command, the Western Route Military Command, and so on... The Northern Route Military Command was the biggest and best-armed force in Manchuria. Led by Kim Jwajin, backed up by men of distinction such as Yi Beomseok and Kim Gyusik, it boasted an arsenal that included machine guns. Meanwhile, the Korean Independence Army, led by Hong Beomdo, was smaller than the Northern Route Military Command but known for its audacity and scored a stunning victory against Japanese troops in a battle at Fengwudong in Manchuria.

Anthem of Hong Beomdo
Wherever Captain Hong goes,
the sun and moon shine bright.
Wherever the Nip army goes,
the sky sheds rain and snow.
Whenever they meet, the Japs go tumbling down.

Their rifles long for enemy blood
Their cannons breathe fire
Whenever they meet, the Japs go tumbling down.

The Northern Route Military Command and the Korean Independence Army, under Kim and Hong, respectively, joined forces at the Battle of Qingshanli to defeat Japanese troops. But let's start by going back to the scene of the Battle of Fengwudong.

Victory at Fengwudong

Fengwudong was a Korean village in Wangqingxian County, Manchuria, that lined two sides of a valley between high mountains. Here, the Korean Independence Army led by Hong Beomdo, the Military Directorate under Choe Jindong and the Gungmin Hoegun under An Mu gathered, with Hong as supreme commander, struck camp on a mountain ridge and waited for the Japanese army to arrive.

At dawn on June 7, 1920, Japanese troops appeared at the entrance to the village. A fierce battle began. Suddenly, it started pouring with rain and the valley and mountainsides were soon shrouded in thick fog. Taking advantage of the situation, the Japanese crept up towards the ridge where the independence army camp lay.

Hong hurriedly ordered his men to climb further up the mountain. The rain had grown heavier and was now mixed

Fengwudong battle site
Fengwudong, in Manchuria, was the site of a major victory for Hong Beomdo's Korean Independence Army against the Japanese. The valley now contains a reservoir.

with hailstones, while thunderclaps shook the valley. The independence fighters left their camp, climbed to higher ground and waited.

Finally, a Japanese unit reached the ridge. But their comrades further down the mountain then opened fire on them, mistaking them for Koreans. The Japanese on the ridge returned the friendly fire. Further up the mountain, the independence fighters watched the enemy troops shooting each other as they awaited Hong's next order.

At last, the rain stopped and the sun came out. Hong aimed his gun at the Japanese commander and pulled the trigger. A hunter by profession, he never missed. When the commander went down, the independence fighters all opened fire.

With their commander gone, the Japanese troops beat a hasty retreat. They had lost some 600 men and the independence fighters had won a resounding victory. This was the now-famous Battle of Fengwudong.

Qinghshanli: the independence fighters' finest hour

After the Battle of Fengwudong, Hong Beomdo's Korean Independence Army headed for the forests to the west of Mt. Baekdusan. The units of An Mu and Choe Jindong and Kim Jwajin's Northern Route Military Command, which had been at Xidapogou in Wangqingxian County, all headed the same way as Hong's men. News had reached them that the Japanese army had begun a large operation to put down Korean independence fighters.

When the Korean forces came together at Helongxian County, to the west of Mt. Baekdusan, Hong, Kim and An held a meeting to discuss ways of responding to the Japanese army's increasingly harsh campaign to wipe them out. One option was to leave Manchuria and cross into the Soviet Union, which was helping Korean independence fighters at the time. The commanders planned to receive weapons and food from Joseon's giant socialist neighbor while preparing there for a long-term war against Japan.

While the Korean forces gathered near

Weapons used at Qingshanli
The Northern Route Military Command was the biggest and best-armed independence army. This photo shows rifles and ammunition used by its men.

Mt. Baekdusan, Japan began its operation to wipe them out.

"The Korean armies have gathered in Helongxian," cried Major-General Masahiko Azuma, commander of the Japanese forces. "This is the perfect chance to crush them all. We can't afford to miss it!"

The Battle of Qingshanli
Qingshanli, in Manchuria's Helongxian County, is home to the thickly-wooded valley in which this battle took place. In fact, the term "Battle of Qingshanli" refers to about ten big and small clashes that took place in the area from October 21 to 26, 1920.
–Independence Hall of Korea

Eventually, a Japanese infantry company entered Baiyunping Valley at around eight o'clock in the morning on October 21, 1920. The forces of the Northern Route Military Command were lying in wait on each side of the valley. In a soft but resolute voice, Kim Jwajin gave them their orders:

"Don't move yet! Wait until all the Japs are in the valley. Don't make a sound, and they're ours!"

The next few minutes seemed like an eternity. Finally, the last of the Japanese troops marched into the valley.

"Fire!"

The independence fighters broke cover in a chorus of gunfire. In an instant, the silent valley was filled with an earsplitting cacophony of shouts, screams, explosions and the rattle of machine guns. The ambush mowed down the Japanese in no time — it was an outstanding success. But Kim now warned his men:

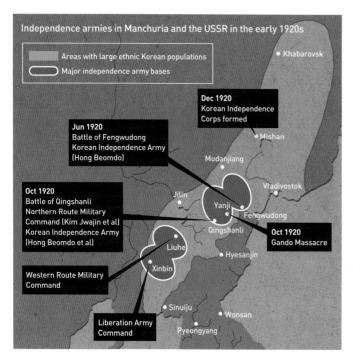

Areas with large ethnic Korean populations

Major independence army bases

• Khabarovsk

Dec 1920
Korean Independence
Corps formed

• Mishan

Jun 1920
Battle of Fengwudong
Korean Independence Army
(Hong Beomdo)

Mudanjiang

• Vladivostok

Jilin

Yanji

Fengwudong

Oct 1920
Battle of Qingshanli
Northern Route Military
Command (Kim Jwajin et al)
Korean Independence Army
(Hong Beomdo et al)

Qingshanli

Oct 1920
Gando Massacre

Liuhe

• Hyesanjin

**Western Route Military
Command**

Xinbin

• Sinuiju

• Wonsan

**Liberation Army
Command**

Pyeongyang

Independence armies were concentrated in areas with large ethnic Korean populations. Leading forces included Manchuria's Northern Route Military Command, Western Route Military Command, Korean Independence Army and Liberation Army Command.

"Soon, their main units will arrive. We have to stay focused: the most important battles are still to come. But we'll win, whatever it takes!"

This episode, now known as the Battle of Baiyunping, was the first of some ten battles that took place in the Qingshanli area over the next six days. These big and small clashes are known collectively as the Battle of Qingshanli. The alliance led by Hong Beomdo, Kim Jwajin and Choe Jindong fought ferociously and ended up victorious.

Some people claim the Battle of Qingshanli was fought only by Kim Jwajin's Northern Route Military Command. But the Korean alliance included Hong Beomdo's Korean Independence Army and several others, even though it's true that Kim Jwajin's men played an important role.

Incensed by its successive defeats at Fengwudong and Qingshanli, the Japanese army went on an arson spree, burning down the homes and schools of ethnic Koreans living in the Gando (Jiandao) area of Manchuria. Many innocent people lost their lives, in an incident that became known as the Gando Massacre or the Gyeongsin Disaster, *gyeongsin* being the calendar name of 1920.

The hunter and the aristocrat

Hong Beomdo and Kim Jwajin, both brilliant independence fighters, came from very different backgrounds. Hong, born in 1868 into a poor family in Pyongyang, had tried his hand at all manner of tough jobs: casual laborer, farmhand, hunter, and miner. He joined a righteous army at the age of twenty-eight and soon gained a fearsome reputation among the Japanese for his skills as a marksman, a legacy of his hunting background. After the annexation, Hong traveled to Manchuria and became an independence fighter, quickly emerging as a leader of men who joined him for his reputation.

Kim Jwajin was the son of a well-known *yangban* family in Hongseong, Chungcheongnam-do Province. Born in 1889, he was twenty-one years younger than Hong. His pen name was Baegya. After forming a pro-independence group in Joseon,

Longjing, Jiandao
Longjing, a town on the Hailanjiang River in Jiandao, had a large Korean population. Many more Koreans moved there after the March First Movement. It was a center of commerce and of pro-independence activity. This photo was taken in the 1910s.

Kim decided to take up arms and fight the Japanese himself. He, too, moved to Manchuria, where he became commander-in-chief of the Northern Route Military Command and opened a rigorous training camp for independence fighters.

Kim Jwajin (left) and
Hong Beomdo
Those who believed in armed struggle joined independence armies, of which Kim and Hong were leading commanders. The former was shot dead by a fellow Korean in Manchuria, while the latter died later on in Kazakhstan, years after being forcibly relocated by Soviet authorities. Hong is still revered by ethnic Koreans in the Central Asian country.

What happened to Hong and Kim after the Battle of Qingshanli? The former led his unit into the Soviet Union, while the latter headed the same way, then returned to China. After settling in Primorsky Krai, Hong was sent to Kazakhstan in 1937, along with some 180,000 ethnic Koreans forcibly relocated to Central Asia from this region at the time. I'll tell you more about this episode later on. Many descendants of those sent to Central Asia by the Soviet authorities back then still live there today.

Hong died in Kazakhstan in 1943, at the age of seventy-six. Ethnic Koreans in Manchuria and Central Asia still revere him as a hero, while his life story has been made into a novel and performed as plays.

Meanwhile, Kim Jwajin continued his independence struggle after returning to Manchuria, forming a group called the New People's Government. A staunch anti-communist, he fought for independence while keeping his left-wing

Kim Jwajin's birthplace
Born into a *yangban* family, Kim later became an independence army commander. This is his birthplace, in Hongseong-gun County, Chungcheongnam-do Province.

compatriots at arm's length and refusing to collaborate with them. In January, 1930 he was shot dead by a young ethnic Korean, whom many thought to be a communist.

You may find it hard to believe that Kim was killed by a fellow Korean after devoting himself to the fight for independence. At the time, however, a schism existed between independence fighters in favor of communism and those against it. Japan exploited this division as best it could, provoking several fights. Though all independence fighters ultimately shared the same goal of national liberation, their ideological disputes gradually grew worse. And the fact that some Koreans in their midst were working as spies for Japan made it even harder for them to trust each other. Kim Jwajin's tragic death took place against this background.

Countless other Koreans traveled to faraway lands to risk their lives fighting for

Stele commemorating Kim Jwajin
This stele is carved with a poem that expresses Kim's feelings while leading an independence army against Japanese forces. Its title, *Danjang-ji tong*, refers to agony as intense as disembowelment. The stele stands at the Independence Hall of Korea in Cheonan, Chungcheongnam-do Province.

Cenotaph to unknown fallen independence fighters
This monument was erected in 2002 to commemorate the unknown dead of the independence struggle. It stands in Seoul National Cemetry.

independence in the thirty-five years of Japanese colonial rule. Even as they died in battle on the plains and in the mountains of Manchuria, they held onto the dream of freedom for their lost country.

These lyrics from *Jeonsiga*, a favorite song of the independence fighters, offer a taste of their passionate patriotism:

On we march, resolute,
across the endless Manchurian plains.
Resigned to lives of hardship,
shedding blood and tears day after day.

Away from our families and friends

through years of lonely struggle,

we'll fight for our homeland of 5,000 years

and win back eternal freedom for our children.

Hidden heroes of independence

The independence armies could not have won the victories they did without the help of many nameless heroes: the ethnic Koreans living in Manchuria. These expatriates, who had moved north of the Joseon border when life at home became impossible, made a living by farming the Manchurian land. An indispensable source of help to Joseon's independence armies, they provided food, hiding places and intelligence about the Japanese army.

As a result, the Japanese in Manchuria burned several ethnic Korean villages to the ground, branding them independence army bases, and shot many Koreans on sight.

A Korean farm in ruins
Japanese killed many ethnic Koreans living in Manchuria and burned down their homes and schools on the pretext of suppressing independence armies. But their will for independence remained undiminished.

Yi Hwarim, the female general

Men and women fought alongside each other in the struggle against Japan. Independence armies counted many female soldiers in their ranks, just like the righteous armies before them. One of the best-known is Yi Hwarim, a general in the Korean Volunteer Army.

Yi was born in Pyeongyang in 1905 under the name Yi Chunsil. At the age of twenty-six, while studying to become a kindergarten teacher, she decided to travel to China and fight with an independence army instead. Yi had worked under Kim Gu as a secretary for the Provisional Government in Shanghai; she now left, entered university in China and studied law and medicine. Yi joined the Korean Volunteer Army and took part in a series of fierce battles that took her as far as the Taihangshan Mountains, deep in western China.

Many peaks in the Taihangshan range exceed 2,000 meters in height. There is nowhere to grow crops in this harsh landscape, and the soldiers of the Korean Volunteer Army had a hard time staying alive. Yi gathered her fellow female fighters, picked wild parsley growing on the mountainsides and made kimchi. They also made flour by boiling and grinding acorns. One day, while picking plants to eat, she composed a song set to the tune of *Doraji*, a popular Korean folk song, and taught it to the others. They gave a performance at lunchtime:

Parsley, parsley, oh, wild parsley
growing in the valleys of Taihangshan.
Just two plants plucked from the ground
fill even the biggest basket.
Oh, how good you are.
Pluck pluck pluck, dig dig dig.
It's all part of the revolution!

After Korean liberation, Yi stayed in China and kept studying medicine, considering it a skill badly needed in her liberated homeland. In the end, though, she stayed in China and became a doctor. Yi served in several official positions in Beijing's municipal traffic and hygiene bureaus, then died in 1999. From her youthful twenties to the late autumn of her nineties, she spent her life as an anti-Japanese warrior on the Chinese continent, utterly devoted to her country.

Female soldiers of the Korean Volunteer Army
This independence army was formed in China in 1938, under the leadership of Kim Wonbong.

A variety of independence armies were active in China and Russia throughout the colonial period: the Korean Revolutionary Army under Yang Seobong (also known as Yang Sebong); the Korean Independence Party Army under Yi Cheongcheon (also known as Ji Jeongcheon); the Korean Volunteer Army, in which Yi Hwarim served; the Northeast Anti-Japanese United Army; and the Korean Liberation Army, the armed force of the Provisional Government, to name but a few. Each army had a different ideology and set of beliefs. Yi Hwarim's Korean Volunteer Army and the Manchuria-based Northeast Anti-Japanese United Army believed in socialism; the KVA fought alongside the Communist Party of China under Mao Zedong against the Japanese in the Taihangshan Mountains. The Northeast Anti-Japanese United Army, meanwhile, was an alliance between Korean and Chinese forces; its Korean division was commanded by Kim Ilsung.

Though the many independence armies fighting Japan espoused different ideologies, they all risked their lives on the battlefield in the struggle to liberate their country and people.

CHAPTER 6

Bang Jeonghwan and Children's Day

To My Young Comrades
Watch the sun as it rises and sets.
Treat not only adults but each other with respect.
Don't write or draw pictures in the toilet, or on the walls.
Leave flowers and plants unpicked, and be kind to animals.
Give your seats to adults on the tram and the train.

세계어린이운동발상지

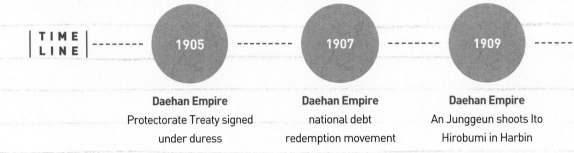

TIME LINE

1905
Daehan Empire
Protectorate Treaty signed
under duress

1907
Daehan Empire
national debt
redemption movement

1909
Daehan Empire
An Junggeun shoots Ito
Hirobumi in Harbin

"Fly, bird, up into the blue sky··· Today is Children's Day, when the world belongs to us."

These lyrics are from Korea's well-known Children's Day Song. *Today, every Korean child looks forward to Children's Day, a time when the country's youngsters eat all kinds of delicious food, receive the presents they've wanted all year, and play all day long without being told to study.*

You'll hear some people saying that children are so spoiled nowadays that there's no need for a specially designated Children's Day. And it's true that you often now see children with cases of so-called "prince complex" or "princess complex," when their parents have given them absolutely everything they want.

When Children's Day was first created, though, things were completely different. This was an age in which children obeyed adults without question. And many children from poor families were abandoned by their parents, or forced to do hard labor in factories. Children's Day was introduced in order to safeguard the most basic rights of children, and to help develop their feelings of patriotism. It was about much more than the day of fun and treats we know today.

Let's take a closer look at the origins of this public holiday.

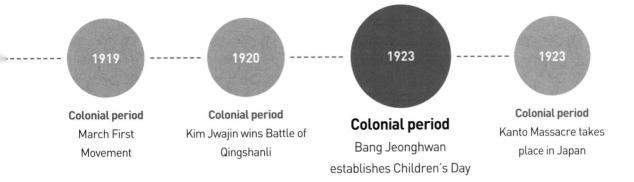

1919

Colonial period

March First
Movement

1920

Colonial period

Kim Jwajin wins Battle of
Qingshanli

1923

Colonial period

Bang Jeonghwan
establishes Children's Day

1923

Colonial period

Kanto Massacre takes
place in Japan

Bang Jeonghwan was studying abroad at Toyo University in Tokyo. Whenever he met his friends, he would try to persuade them.

"Surely bringing up and educating future generations is the most important thing," he would say. "We may be under the control of another country, but the future lies in our children's hands — don't you think they should be able to enjoy their country and their culture to the full?" He and his friends decided to form a group to campaign on behalf of Joseon's youngsters. On the suggestion of Bang's friend, Yun Geugyeong, they called it the Rainbow Society, a name that, in addition to its bright connotations, also called to mind the colorful traditional costumes worn by children on public holidays.

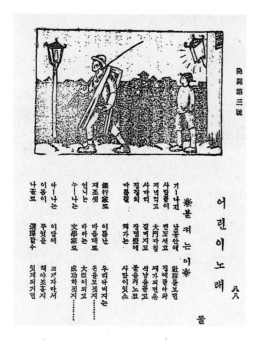

'Eorini norae'
These song lyrics contain Bang's first use of the word *eorini*. He titled his translation of a foreign poem *Eorini norae* ("Children's Song"); it was published in 1920 in the magazine *Gaebyeok*.

Yun himself went on to become a composer and wrote Bandal ("Half-Moon") a famous children's song that includes the lyrics, "A white canoe sailing through the galaxy in the blue sky." At the time, however, he was studying not composition but instrumental music.

Children's Day: May 1

At the same time as they formed the Rainbow Society, Bang and his friends decided to create "Children's Day" and hold an event to mark it. The date was set for May 1, 1923, in a Cheondoist meeting hall—note the difference with contemporary Children's Day, which is held on May 5.

On May 1, 1923, the first Children's Day event took place. It was organized by the Youth Movement Association, an umbrella organization formed by some forty groups including the Rainbow Society, the Cheondogyo Children's Association, the Buddhist Children's Association and the Peninsular Children's Army. A noisy event ensued; when it was over, four groups of fifty children each made their way around Seoul, delivering 120,000 pamphlets publicizing Children's Day. The pamphlets carried this message:

The Children's Day Pledge

Today is Children's Day, a new holiday symbolizing hope. Our hope is simple: to offer children a good upbringing. ... Children are newer beings than adults. We need to see our sons and daughters not as our possessions, but as the people that make up a new generation. ... Treat children even better than you treat adults. ... Never bully a child. ... Always make your children's lives happy. ... Spare no praise as you bring them up.

Children's day procession
When the Children's Day event was over, youngsters paraded through the streets handing out leaflets advertising Children's Day and cheering as they walked. Adults were puzzled and amused by the scene.

Children's Day slogans
The first Children's Day ceremony was held on May 1, 1923. In 1928, the date was changed to the first Sunday of May. The slogans on this flier read "Take care of children for a better society!" "Let's find hope again!" and "Let's build a brighter future!"
–Independence Hall of Korea

The Children's Day celebration grew more popular each year. In 1924, the second year it was held, some 1,000 children attended. This time, the event continued from May 1 to 4 and included events such as the "mothers' competition" and the "fathers' competition." Jo Pungyon, who attended the celebration as a second-grade elementary student, later went on to become a writer. Here, he recalls the event:

"We didn't go far, just from Jae-dong crossroads down to Anguk-dong, then to Jongno, and back again when we got to Jongno 3-ga. But all the adults came out into the street to see what was going on. We loved being the center of their attention. When the leaders cheered from somewhere in the middle of the procession, we all cheered too. It was great fun seeing the adults bewildered by such an unfamiliar scene."

From 1928, Children's Day was shifted to the first Sunday of May. This change aimed to avoid an overlap with Labor Day, also on May 1, and ensured that as many people as possible would be free to take part. Japanese authorities banned Children's Day in 1937. After liberation, however, it was revived, and celebrated on May 5, 1946. Oh, and it only became an official public holiday much later, in 1975.

Bronze statue of Bang Jeonghwan
This statue of Bang sits in Children's Grand Park in Neung-dong, Seoul. "Invest ten years in your children for the sake of the nation's future," Bang suggested. He was a true friend of children, dedicating his life to them amid the poverty and hunger of the colonial period.

'Neulgeuni,' 'jeolmeuni,' 'eorini'

It's worth noting that Bang Jeonghwan was also the first person to bring about widespread use of *eorini*, a pure Korean word for young children that comes from the verb *eorida* ("to be young or little"). Until then, most people had used the Sino-Korean words *adong* and *sonyeon* to talk about young children. Bang suggested using the word *eorini* in order that young children be regarded as real people, too. Koreans already used the words *neulgeuni* for old people and *jeolmeuni* for young adults, both of which also come from pure Korean verbs meaning "old" and "young," respectively. Bang reasoned that using the word *eorini* held young children in higher esteem and would help them grow into well-rounded adults. Such is the power of language, which Bang held to be mightier than the sword or the gun.

Bang's belief in respect for children was strongly influenced by Donghak ideology, according to which people and Heaven are one and the same. As you'll hopefully recall, Donghak was a religion founded by Choe Jeu that became known as Cheondoism in 1905. Son Byeonghui, one of the popular representatives that organized the March First Movement, was the third leader of the Cheondoist faith, after Choe Jeu and Choe Sihyeong; Bang Jeonghwan was the husband of Son's third daughter.

Children in hunger and poverty

Bang constantly urged adults to give their children plenty of praise, and to make sure they were washed and had their hair cut properly. These things might seem obvious to us now, but they were highly unfamiliar concepts to most people at the time. Joseon was a very poor country; even scraping a basic living was hard enough, leaving people with little time to think of much else. Here's an illustration of the kind of lives people led in those days:

It was 1933, in a rural village in Deogwon, Hamgyeongnam-do Province. In a shabby house by the side of the road, a family of five sat listlessly, eating something. All of them had

Children at a straw bag market
These youngsters are selling straw
sacks. Bang Jeonghwan tried to
bring hope to children struggling
to survive in the face of poverty.

purple, swollen eyelids and were covered in blisters. They were too exhausted even to speak. When a visitor asked what they were eating, the father answered in barely audible whisper that their hunger had driven them to make a mixture of millet, rice bran, soy beans and sesame pulp. When this was all gone, he said, they would have to eat radish or kudzu roots.

Just then, one of the children started crying and complaining of a stomach ache. Tut-tutting, the father carried him out. The curious visitor followed them outside, where he found the father poking at his son's backside with a stick about a foot long. The boy was severely constipated. Soon afterwards, the son came back inside, crying in his father's arms. "Adults can eat sorghum, but children can't digest it," the father explained. "They cry because their stomachs hurt.

Shantytown hut
Around 1936, Seoul's slums were home to some 110,000 people: more than one in every six of the city's approximately 600,000 inhabitants.

The life of a laborer
By the late 1920s, Joseon was home to some 200,000 workers. Around thirty-five percent were women, while some 7.5 percent were children. Most of them worked at Japanese-owned factories, in difficult and dangerous conditions.

It's the same with rice bran."

Seoul, just like the countryside, was the scene of much poverty. Its poorest citizens were those who had come to the city when life in the countryside became impossible for them. When they reached the capital, they would build themselves ramshackle mud huts on mountainsides, by streams or under bridges.

In those days, the center of Seoul was filling with impressive Western-style buildings such as the headquarters of the Government-General, its streets busy with trams and cars. Only slightly further out, however, the city spread into shantytowns full of dirty, tumbledown shacks.

The slum dwellers lived off gruel boiled up from various plant roots and tree bark. Their children frequently suffered from malnutrition and grew sick. They had one set of clothes to get them through the cold winter, and one duvet for the whole family to huddle under at night. Many children went to work in factories to scrape any meager wage they could, unable to even dream of going to school. In most big factories during the colonial period, around a quarter of the workers were children.

Most children in the colonial period, then, led lives not of studying and playing but of poverty and starvation. This was the background to Bang Jeonghwan's campaign to create Children's Day and to value and respect the nation's youngsters. Living in poverty was not an excuse to neglect children, he argued, but all the more reason to give them the best possible upbringing and fill them with hope for a better future. In many ways, Bang's fight for children was actually a consciousness raising campaign aimed at adults.

'Eorini: a magazine for children

In addition to creating Children's Day, one of Bang Jeonghwan's greatest achievements was publishing *Eorini* ("Youngster") magazine. We have all sorts of magazines for children nowadays, but nothing of the kind existed back then. *Eorini* contained stories, songs and poems for children. Many of Korea's best-known children's writers today, such as

'Eorini' magazine
Large newspaper advertisements heralded the inaugural issue of *Eorini* magazine in 1923. "How can you raise your children better? *Eorini* is the first step. ... Read it yourself first, then read it to your children." Who could refuse such a tempting advertisement?
–Headquarters of Cheondoism

Yun Seokjung, Yi Wonsu, Gang Socheon, Ma Haesong and Choe Sunae, made their debuts in *Eorini* at this time.

Bang Jeonghwan died in 1931, aged just thirty-three. His relentless hard work had taken a heavy toll on his health, and he succumbed to kidney disease and high blood pressure. His text, *Eorin dongmudeul-ege* ("To My Young Comrades"), still resonates more than eighty years after his death:

To My Young Comrades
Watch the sun as it rises and sets.

When will independence come?

Yun Seokjung is well-known for a nursery rhyme he wrote about throwing stones into the water. Another of his works is a children's poem called *Dongnip* ("Independence"):

By the side of the road was an old underground shelter.
Inside, homeless people had laid down straw mats
and made it their home.
One small child peered out, like a swallow's chick
and asked a passerby:
When will independence come?

It seems the child in the poem thought that independence would bring a better life. During the colonial period, countless children lived like this one, sleeping on straw mats and fighting hunger every day. Many of them went on to become the grandparents of today's young Koreans.

Treat not only adults but each other with respect.

Don't write or draw pictures in the toilet, or on the walls.

Leave flowers and plants unpicked, and be kind to animals.

Give your seats to adults on the tram and the train.

Keep your mouth closed and make sure you stand straight.

Children's Day was made to offer youngsters in the colonial period hope for a brighter, healthier future. If you have younger siblings or even children of your own, why not tell them about the origins of this public holiday? It's an important part of Korean history, after all.

Bang Jeonghwan's 'Message to Adults'
"Don't look down on children; look up to them. Speak to them politely but always gently. Wash them and cut their hair regularly. Make sure they have enough sleep and exercise. ..." Bang published this text to mark the first ever Children's Day. It is carved on a stele that stands in the grounds of the Independence Hall of Korea.

세계어린이운동발상지

Memorial to the cradle of the world children's movement
This memorial was placed outside the Cheondogyo Central Temple in Seoul in 2000. Its inscription reads, "Adults must not suppress children. The people of thirty or forty years ago must not hold back those of thirty or forty years into the future."

Kim Sowol's 'Azaleas'

When you're sick of me and you leave,

don't think I'll try and stop you.

No, I'll pick myself an armful of azaleas

and scatter them across your path as you leave.

You can give them a good trampling

with every step you take from my door.

So leave when you've had enough

as long as you don't expect me to cry.

Kim Sowol's 'Azaleas'
Born in Guseong, Pyeonganbuk-do Province, Kim studied in Japan before returning to Joseon after the Great Kanto Earthquake. His attempt at running a business ended in failure and he took his own life at the age of thirty-three. Kim left the 1925 poetry anthology *Azaleas*.

Many people today know these words as the lyrics to a song by a well-known singer. And it's true, they are. But they were originally written in the form of a poem, during the colonial period, by a poet called Kim Sowol (his original name was Kim Jeongsik).

Kim also wrote a number of other beautiful poems, including *Sanyuhwa* ("Mountain Flowers"), *Yejeon-e micheo mollasseoyo* ("I Never Even Realized"), *Meon hunnal* ("The Distant Future"), *Eomma-ya, nuna-ya* ("Mom, Sister") and *Mot ijeo* ("I Can't Forget"). His works are full of sadness, yet uncomplicated, which is why so many of them have been taken as lyrics for pop songs.

Like Bang Jeonghwan, Kim Sowol studied in Japan. He attended Tokyo University of Commerce, but abandoned his studies and returned to Joseon after the Great Kanto Earthquake. Many young Koreans went to study in Japan during the colonial period. Like the old saying, "To catch a tiger, you have to go into its cave first," these students believed there were things they had to learn from Japan. After all, their colonial occupier was ahead of Joseon in adopting Western culture at the time. These students played an important role in bringing new ideas and culture into Joseon via Japan.

CHAPTER 7

The Kanto Massacre and forced relocation

In September, 1937, fourteen years after the Kanto Massacre, an order was given for the forcible relocation of ethnic Koreans living in Primorsky Krai. The reason given was that they had the potential to become spies for Japan, and therefore had to be sent somewhere far away.

With barely a day's notice, the Koreans were put onto trains and sent away. They had no idea where they were headed, or how long the journey would take.

TIME
LINE

Daehan Empire
Protectorate Treaty signed
under duress

1905

Daehan Empire
national debt
redemption movement

1907

Daehan Empire
An Junggeun shoots Ito
Hirobumi in Harbin

1909

The Japanese colonial period saw an exodus of Koreans. They migrated to places such as Chinese Manchuria, eastern Russia's maritime Primorsky Krai region and Japan. Why? Because they needed work. Joseon's poorest citizens, squeezed even tighter under the exploitative colonial regime, left for unfamiliar lands in search of ways to survive. They worked hard to build better lives in their new homes, cultivating wild land or finding work in factories.

Many of those who went abroad ending up meeting terrible deaths simply because of their nationality. Even today, their fates remain widely unknown.

What's the point of digging up painful episodes from the past, you might think. Isn't it the future that counts? Of course—but you have to understand the past if you want to manage the future properly. Past, present and future are all closely connected.

Today I'm going to tell you about the Kanto Massacre and the forced relocation of ethnic Koreans from far-eastern Russia to Central Asia. These episodes often evade the spotlight of history, but you really should be aware of them.

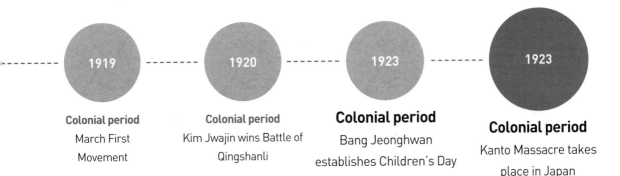

1919	1920	1923	1923
Colonial period	Colonial period	**Colonial period**	**Colonial period**
March First Movement	Kim Jwajin wins Battle of Qingshanli	Bang Jeonghwan establishes Children's Day	Kanto Massacre takes place in Japan

September 1, 1923, was a Saturday. In Tokyo, it had been raining all morning. At around midday, after the rain had stopped, a massive earthquake began. The quake was so powerful that it instantly reduced Tokyo, and surrounding cities such as Yokohama, to piles of rubble. This devastating event is known today as the Great Kanto Earthquake.

Japan was plunged into chaos. Throughout the region, people sobbed in grief as they pulled dead family members out of collapsed houses. But then, a series of strange rumors began spreading. Koreans, it was alleged, were going on the rampage, setting off bombs,

Earthquake damage
The Great Kanto Earthquake flattened Tokyo and the surrounding area in an instant. Kamakura, a city about an hour by train from the capital, was destroyed, and many of its inhabitants killed.

Great Kanto Earthquake
The quake killed and injured countless people. But Japan blamed Koreans for the disaster and began slaughtering them indiscriminately. The number of Koreans killed is still not known for certain. Other Koreans were mobilized in the recovery effort. Though they avoided death, their work was grueling.

poisoning wells, starting fires and killing Japanese.

The Japanese army and police began hunting down Koreans and killing them on sight. Ordinary citizens joined the hunt, forming militias of their own. Armed with knives, bamboo spears, sickles and whatever else they could get their hands on, these vigilante groups hacked to death any Koreans they came across. They burned the bodies, threw them into rivers or buried them in unmarked graves. Children and even pregnant women were shown no mercy. Though nobody can determine the precise number of deaths, it is known to be somewhere in the region of 6,600. Most of their bodies have not been found. To the Japanese, the Great Kanto Earthquake was a natural disaster; to Koreans in Japan, it was also a time of genocide. This episode is often known as the Kanto Massacre.

Koreans become scapegoats

Did Koreans really go around starting fires and poisoning wells when the earthquake struck? No. So who or what started these rumors? Amazingly enough, it was the Japanese government. As soon as the quake occurred, the home minister and the chief commissioner of police issued a nationwide statement in the name of the director of the Bureau of Public Warnings:

"Koreans are taking advantage of the earthquake in the Tokyo region to achieve nefarious aims, including starting fires in various places. Some are currently carrying bombs

Koreans slaughtered in Japan
Unable to pick out Koreans by sight, Japanese vigilante groups stopped people and ordered them to talk. Those who could not speak fluent Japanese were killed.

Crown Prince Hirohito inspects the earthquake zone
The Japanese heir to the throne visits devastated Ueno Park in Tokyo on September 15, a fortnight after the quake.

and spilling petroleum around central Tokyo. ... Please conduct a thorough crackdown on these acts by Koreans."

Martial law was declared in the Tokyo area, while the government went as far as appealing to the Japanese public to form militias and defend itself.

Why on earth did the Japanese government concoct such a lie? The country's leaders were looking for a pretext to declare martial law in order to calm public sentiment, which had hit rock bottom after the earthquake, and to restore order. When they failed to find a good enough excuse, they decided to fabricate a false rumor about rampaging Koreans instead. Put simply, they created scapegoats in order to gain control amid the public panic and disorder created by the quake.

Most of the Koreans murdered in the Kanto Massacre were poor laborers who had made their way to Japan to find work. Many of them didn't speak very good Japanese. Not only Koreans but a considerable number of Japanese opponents of the government were killed in the violence that erupted at this time.

The Kanto Massacre was the result of Japanese politicians taking advantage of a natural disaster to hold onto power and sacrificing expatriate Koreans in the process. Nonetheless, the Japanese government to this day refuses to even state exactly what happened at the time, let alone issue an apology to those who lost their lives. Sadly, even Koreans today don't show much interest in the terrible deaths of their ancestors in Japan ninety years ago.

180,000 ethnic Koreans sent to Central Asia

You may not be too familiar with the Union of Soviet Socialist Republics, often known as the Soviet Union, but people of my age remember it well. As its full name suggests, the Soviet Union was a socialist state. It was dominated by Russia, the biggest country in it. Koreans had been living in Primorsky Krai, Russia's far-eastern maritime province, since the late-Joseon period—long before the Soviet Union was formed in 1922.

The Soviet Union and Primorsky Krai
The Soviet Union was a huge country, stretching from the eastern end of Eurasia, across Central Asia and all the way to Europe. Primorsky Krai, its eastern maritime province, shares a short border with the Korean Peninsula, lying just across the Dumangang, the peninsula's northernmost river. This Russian province was home to many Koreans.

In September, 1937, fourteen years after the Kanto Massacre, an order was given for the forcible relocation of ethnic Koreans living in Primorsky Krai. The reason given was that they had the potential to become spies for Japan, and therefore had to be sent somewhere far away.

With barely a day's notice, the Koreans were put onto trains and sent away. They had no idea where they were headed, or how long the journey would take. 180,000 of them were forcibly relocated this way. Among them was Hong Beomdo, hero of the Battle of Fengwudong.

Koreans are herded onto trains
Around 180,000 Koreans living in Primorsky Krai were forcibly located one day without warning. They had no idea where they were heading as they watched the endless plains of Siberia pass by the train window.

On the trains, four or five families crammed into every compartment. There was just one window. The days were swelteringly hot and the nights freezing. Whenever the train stopped, everyone got out and found a patch of land to prepare food and eat. Children went to fetch water, while the men gathered firewood. There were no toilets, so they had to relieve themselves by the railway tracks. The journey lasted more than a month, with no chance to wash; by the end of it, the Koreans' hair and clothes were full of lice. Whenever the train made a brief stop, the women would open the windows and shake their hair, releasing showers of bugs.

Those who fell ill were put on a stretcher and taken away. They never came back. Koreans therefore started hiding the sick instead of reporting them. Children and the elderly were the first to die; when the train made a stop, their families would bury them near the railway tracks. It was a deeply painful journey.

Ma Hakbong's petition
Ma was forcibly relocated at the age of sixteen. His suffering prompted him to write a petition: "Must only Caucasians live well in the Soviet Union? Is it unacceptable for others to enjoy a decent life? ... If we had known how hard life would be here, we would have chosen to die in Primorsky Krai. ..."

Finally, the ordeal came to an end and the Koreans realized where they had arrived: Kazakhstan and Uzbekistan. Desolate landscapes were all that greeted them. They had nowhere to sleep or even unpack their bags. The locals, meanwhile, eyed them with deep suspicion and kept them at distance, assuming they had been banished for committing some terrible crime. Somebody even started a rumor that Koreans were cannibals who liked to eat children.

The forcibly relocated Koreans were set to work on collective farms, where they did their best to cultivate the Central Asian wilderness with picks and shovels. They had no oxen to plow the fields or decent farming equipment, but they doggedly worked at the land with their hand tools. Gradually, the harsh soil turned to fertile farmland, and a crop of rice ripened golden yellow. The Koreans' hard work and

Forced relocation memorial steles
This is where the Koreans forcibly moved to Central Asia by the Soviet authorities spent their first winter. The stele records how they dug tunnels and lived here from October 9, 1937 to April 10 the following year.

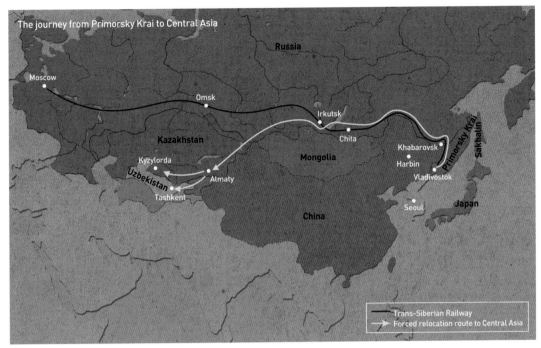

The journey from Primorsky Krai to Central Asia

Russia

Moscow

Omsk

Irkutsk

Kazakhstan

Chita

Khabarovsk

Harbin

Primorsky Krai

Sakhalin

Kyzylorda

Uzbekistan

Almaty

Mongolia

Vladivostok

Tashkent

China

Seoul

Japan

— Trans-Siberian Railway
→ Forced relocation route to Central Asia

outstanding knowledge of rice cultivation more than doubled production.

Koreans relocated from Russia's Maritime Province arrived in Kazakhstan and Uzbekistan, countries around 8,000 kilometers away. Many of their descendants still live there.

Koreans executed on false charges

At almost the same time that the forcible relocations took place, some 2,500 Koreans were framed as Japanese spies or impure elements opposed to the Soviet Union. Some were executed; others went missing and were never seen again. Many Koreans who had migrated to Primorsky Krai after Joseon's annexation by Japan became socialists or joined the Soviet armed forces as a way of fighting for their country's independence. Now, they suddenly found themselves branded spies or impure elements and unjustly put to death. Later on, they were found to be innocent. But that did nothing to make up for the pain that they and their families suffered.

Koreans were not the only people to be forcibly relocated

! Ethnic Koreans left behind in Sakhalin

The island of Sakhalin lies just to the north of Japan's northernmost tip. While it now belongs to Russia, the island was part of Japanese territory during the colonial period. Today, several tens of thousands of ethnic Koreans live there. But how did they end up in such a far-flung place?

Ethnic Koreans in Sakhalin

During the colonial period, Japan opened mines on Sakhalin and sent Koreans to work there. More than 40,000 Korean laborers were forcibly transported to the island. But even worse was to come after Japan's defeat in World War II: Sakhalin became Soviet territory and the Koreans living there were left with nowhere to go. Japan transported its own citizens back to their motherland but left the Koreans behind. All the latter could do was stand in utter frustration as they watched the last Japanese boats set sail. Repatriating them would have required cooperation between Japan, the Soviet Union and Korea, but this was not forthcoming. Most of the Koreans taken to Sakhalin during the colonial period have now died, but their descendants still live there, hundreds of miles from their ancestral homeland. We know very little about them.

in 1937. Iranians, Turks, Kurds and Armenians living in western border regions of the Soviet Union were also sent off to Central Asia and made to work on collective farms. These relocations were enforced with excessive haste and without any preparation or policies to support the new relocated peoples. Their sudden departure had forced the ethnic Koreans of Primorsky Krai to leave their homes, livestock, crops and other possessions behind: everything that they had accumulated through endless, backbreaking work in the harsh Russian landscape.

The Soviet Union relocated the ethnic Koreans of Primorsky Krai in the belief that they might become enemy spies if it went to war with China or Japan. Whatever its reasons, the move merely added to the sorrow of people who had already lost their own country. If Joseon had been a strong, independent state rather than a colony of Japan, it's unlikely that its people would have so easily been forced to move.

Coming home
A project to repatriate ethnic Koreans in Sakhalin began in 1997. Some have come back, while more than 3,000 are still awaiting their turn. All of them are now quite old.

Koreiski
The 180,000 forcibly relocated ethnic Koreans were forced to begin new lives on the desolate plains of Central Asia. But the little-known tale of their immense suffering has been consigned to the back pages of history. Those who were sent by train from Primorsky Krai all those years ago have mostly died, while their descendants remain in Central Asia, no longer able to speak Korean. They are still known by other Russians as Koreiski, meaning "Koreans."

The photo brides of Hawaii

Fifteen-year-old Choe Anna (not a real name) gazed back at the port of Busan as it grew smaller and smaller. She took out the locket that hung around her neck and looked at the photo again. She was sailing to Hawaii to marry the man in the photo. Among her fellow passengers were five other girls on the way to meet their promised husbands. It was 1915 and Joseon had been a colony of Japan for five years.

Sugar plantation laborers
Korean migrant workers in Hawaii rose at four in the morning and worked for ten hours every day. Whenever they were deemed to have stepped even slightly out of line, they were whipped like slaves.

The voyage across the Pacific lasted three whole months. Whenever the girls grew seasick, their guide told them stories of Hawaii. Clothes grow on trees there, he said, and the fruit is so plentiful that it just falls to the ground and rots. There's no need to spend money, so saving is easy.

When the ship finally reached Hawaii, the girls waited for their men to arrive. Choe's fiancé turned up on the fifth day. Unlike the man in the photo, he was a forty-six-year-old sugar cane plantation worker with a deeply wrinkled face and gnarled hands. Some 7,000 Koreans were working on Hawaii's sugar plantations at the time, most of them single men. Getting married was their biggest difficulty, which they would solve by sending photos of themselves to their hometowns back in Korea and having a suitable bride found. This practice was known as "photo marriage." Many men would send photos of themselves taken ten years previously. Some

Photo brides
Photo brides arriving
in Honolulu took
commemorative photos
together before separating
and going off with their
respective new husbands.
These ones all look mature
and optimistic.

even borrowed shots of other, better-looking friends. Brides that crossed the ocean after placing all their trust in a single photo were frequently disappointed once they arrived, but what could they do? More than 1,000 women got married through photo weddings like this. What prompted them to move to faraway Hawaii? Poverty, the desire to earn money and discover a new world, plans to join the independence struggle... their reasons were many. But what they all had in common was a longing to escape poverty and uncertainty and begin new lives.

CHAPTER 8

Sin Chaeho, the father of modern history

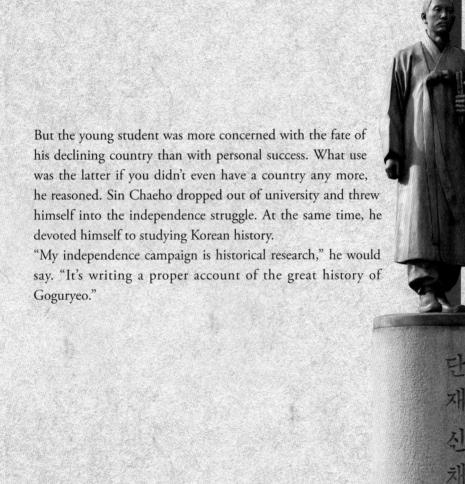

But the young student was more concerned with the fate of his declining country than with personal success. What use was the latter if you didn't even have a country any more, he reasoned. Sin Chaeho dropped out of university and threw himself into the independence struggle. At the same time, he devoted himself to studying Korean history.

"My independence campaign is historical research," he would say. "It's writing a proper account of the great history of Goguryeo."

1931

Colonial period

Sin Chaeho's *Joseon sanggosa* serialized in *Chosun ilbo*

1932

Colonial period

Yi Bongchang and Yun Bonggil attack Japan

1936

Colonial period

Sohn Keechung wins Berlin Olympic marathon

One of my greatest personal heroes is the historian Sin Chaeho. I admire him not just for his outstanding achievements, but because he was a man who put his beliefs into practice. Matching all your thoughts and words with action is not easy. Many people keep them in separate realms, through lack of courage or because they just want an easy life. But Sin was different. As a scholar, an independence activist, a poet and a novelist, he remained consistent from start to finish.

Have you heard the story of how Sin Chaeho washed his face? Even then, he refused to bow his head, instead letting water flow up his sleeves and getting all his clothes soaking wet. Why? To live up to his belief in being "scared of nothing." This famous anecdote wonderfully illustrates Sin's unyielding character. Let's see what his life was like.

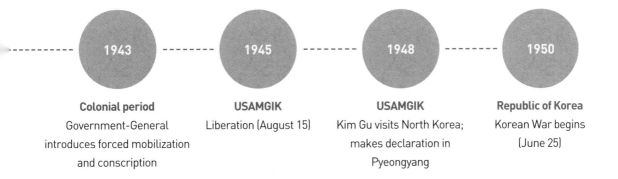

1943

Colonial period
Government-General
introduces forced mobilization
and conscription

1945

USAMGIK
Liberation (August 15)

1948

USAMGIK
Kim Gu visits North Korea;
makes declaration in
Pyeongyang

1950

Republic of Korea
Korean War begins
(June 25)

Today's historians consider Sin Chaeho the father of modern Korean history. Focusing his studies on antiquity, he made a series of unprecedented claims at a time when Japanese scholars dominated historical research.

Japanese academics were taking a fine toothcomb to Korean history in search of ways to justify their country's imperialist ambitions. Japan wanted a firm understanding of its neighbor's history, culture, customs and systems in order to reinforce its colonial grip. This

Sin Chaeho
Sin was renowned for his extreme stubbornness. But everyone agreed that his was an exemplary kind of obstinacy. He was consistent in everything he did, be it studying history or fighting for independence.

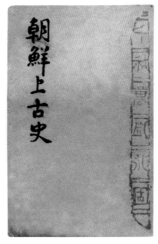

Joseon sanggosa ('An Early History of Korea')
This study of Korean antiquity was one of Sin's major works.

practice is known as colonial historiography and its product as a colonial view of history.

Why study antiquity?

The colonial historiographers claimed it was natural for Joseon to become a colony of Japan, since it had been controlled by foreign powers since long ago and lagged behind its eastern neighbor in many aspects. But Sin disproved each of their arguments, one by one. The first autonomously founded Korean state was Dangun's Gojoseon, he said. And that was followed by Goguryeo. We occupied not only the the Korean Peninsula but wide swathes of Manchuria, too: just look at Goguryeo and Balhae. The four commanderies built by Han, which conquered Gojoseon, were located not on the peninsula but in Manchuria. Baekje extended its power to Liaoxi, the Shandong Peninsula in China, and Japan. And Japan's ancient culture was formed from a mixture of Goguryeo, Baekje and Silla influences.

Sin described Korean history from a totally different perspective to any historian before him, citing new materials. He condemned Kim Chunchu, previously revered as a hero for unifying the Three Kingdoms, for bringing in foreign powers. He argued that the Unified Silla period should instead be regarded as one of two Korean states, Silla and

Colonial historiography
Japan's colonial historiographers contended that their country had ruled parts of the Korean Peninsula during the Three Kingdoms period, and that all development in Korean history had come from outside the peninsula rather than from indigenous efforts. Put simply, they were claiming that Korean history was immobile and devoid of progress. This notion is sometimes called the stagnation theory. As a people, they said, Koreans were lazy, incapable of acting in unity and dependent upon others. This is known as the heteronomy theory—another difficult term for you. The fastidiousness of these colonial historiographers may have been exemplary, but their attitude and motives were reprehensible.

Balhae. And he was particularly fierce in his criticism of the Confucian Korean policy of accepting the role of vassal state to China. Sin claimed that Korea's indigenous ideology was not Confucianism but something he called the "Nangga ideal," a tradition whose roots he traced from the time of Dangun, via Silla's Hwarang system, to the present.

Sin's study of antiquity was aimed at refuting the claims of Japan's colonial historiographers. His books are infused with a powerful sense of love for and pride in his nation. Indeed, his work might even be described as "nationalist historiography."

Embracing new Western theories, Sin claimed that the history of humanity was a process of evolution through certain stages. He described history itself as "the record of a struggle between the ego and the nonego," which, when applied to Joseon, signified a record of the struggle between the Korean nation and other nations.

Nobody had ever described Korean history the way Sin did. He opened a new chapter altogether, which is why he is often called the father of modern Korean history.

Goguryeo historiography becomes part of the independence struggle

Sin Chaeho was born in 1880 in Eonam-ri, a village in

Sin Chaeho's birthplace
Sin was born and lived here until his father died, at which point he went to live with his grandfather in Cheongwon, Chungcheongbuk-do Province. The building in the photo is a reproduction of the original house. It stands in Eonam-dong, a neighborhood of Daejeon.

Chungcheongnam-do Province. Among his ancestors was Sin Sukju, a renowned scholar from the time of King Sejong. Sin's family was now very poor and struggled to get through each day on a bowl or two of gruel. But despite his difficult background, the boy was a brilliant student. He attended the village school where his grandfather taught, studying Chinese and Confucianism, memorizing classics such as *The Analects* and *Mencius* and enjoying classical Chinese novels such as Sanguozhi (Records of the Three Kingdoms) and *Shuihuzhi* (The Water Margin).

Sin was oblivious to everything but study. His family's poverty left him thin and feeble-looking, while he dressed shabbily and never showed much sign of feeling. His friends and fellow villagers found him strange and somewhat dim. When Sin's grandfather got wind of this, he sat him down for a concerned talk.

"Everyone says you're a strange, absent-minded boy," he said. "Why do you think that is?"

"Who knows?" answered Sin, sounding unconcerned. "I'm not particularly interested in people like that."

Sin's character was such that he absorbed himself totally in studying whatever captured his attention. He retained this trait throughout his life.

In 1898, when he was nineteen years old, Sin entered Sungkyunkwan University. Graduates of this prestigious state institution were practically guaranteed success in life: all Sin had to do was devote himself to his beloved study in preparation for wealth and honor later on.

But the young student was more concerned with the fate of his declining country than with personal success. What use was the latter if you didn't even have a country any more, he reasoned. He dropped out of university and threw himself into the independence struggle. At the same time, he devoted himself to studying Korean history.

"My independence campaign is historical research," he would say. "It's writing a proper account of the great history of Goguryeo."

Sin explores Goguryeo ruins in Manchuria
Sin left Joseon just before the annexation and traveled to
Manchuria, where he explored various Goguryeo historic sites.
He worked hard to revise the history of this ancient Korean state.

A thorough nationalist and patriot

Immediately before the Daehan Empire's annexation, Sin
fled to China to escape Japanese persecution. Though he left
behind almost all his belongings, he made sure to take a copy
of *Dongsa gangmok* ("Annotated Account of Korean History"),
a book by Joseon historian An Jeongbok. One of An's
descendants had lent the precious book to Sin, but Sin now
chose to take it to China rather than return it. He had never
coveted material possessions, but it seems he was simply
unable to part with *Dongsa gangmok*. It frequently served him

as a reference source.

Sin traveled around Manchuria and Primorsky Krai, researching his nation's history. He explored the former territories of Goguryeo and Balhae, in Manchuria, climbed Mt. Baekdusan and saw the Gwanggaeto Stele for himself. The Goguryeo ruins left him deeply impressed. "Seeing these places just once is better than reading Kim Busik's *Samguk sagi* ten times!" he said.

Sin Chaeho in Shanghai
Sin stands on the left in this picture. He is wearing Chinese clothes to disguise his Korean nationality.

Sin was notoriously stubborn. At one point, he made a living by contributing articles to Chinese newspapers such as *Beijing ribao* (Beijing Daily) and *Zhonghua bao* (China Times). Whenever they left out or changed certain words without his permission, he would fly into a rage and swear never to write for them again. One comment from Yi Kwangsu, an up-and-coming novelist at the time, serves to illustrate Sin's unbending character:

"He was a thoroughly upright man. It seemed that if you hit him anywhere on his body, you'd hear the sound *minjok* ["nation"], or that if you stabbed him, patriotic blood would flow from the wound."

Sin contributed to the founding of the Provisional

Government in Shanghai, but vehemently opposed suggestions that Syngman Rhee be made its prime minister. Rhee had asked the United States to govern Joseon in a trusteeship arrangement after independence was achieved; making such a man prime minister was absurd, Sin argued.

"Yi Wanyong betrayed the Daehan Empire," he shouted. "But Syngman Rhee wants to betray a country that doesn't even exist yet!"

When Syngman Rhee was elected not prime minister but president of the Provisional Government, Sin left it altogether.

Taking up arms for independence

After quitting the Provisional Government, Sin came to believe that fighting the Japanese directly was the only remaining path to independence. *Joseon hyeongmyeong seoneon* ("The Declaration of the Korean Revolution"), which he wrote at this time, shows how he was thinking. Sin wrote the declaration on behalf of the Righteous Patriots Corps, at the request of his close friend and corps leader Kim Wonbong:

"If Joseon is to survive, the rogue state Japan must be kicked out. Revolution is the only way to achieve this. Without one, Japan can never be driven out of Joseon…"

Sin created a group called the Beijing Conference of the

Righteous Patriots Corps leader Kim Wonbong
The Righteous Patriots Corps was formed in 1919 to fight the Japanese. Its leader was Kim Wonbong. The corps performed missions such as assassinating Japanese officials and military officers, and destroying police stations. It later became the National Revolutionary Party. Yi Yuksa, the poet who wrote the well-known work *Cheongpodo* ("Green Grapes"), with its memorable opening line, "July in my hometown, when the green grapes ripen on the vine," was also a member.

Eastern Anarchist Federation in order to put his ideas into practice. On a fundraising trip to Taiwan, while pretending to be Chinese, he was caught by the Japanese police. Sentenced to ten years behind bars, Sin found himself incarcerated in Lushun, the prison that had earlier held An Junggeun.

Sin died of a brain hemorrhage in Lushun in February, 1936. He was fifty-seven.

"When I die, cremate me and scatter my ashes over the sea so the Nips can never walk over my dead body," he used to say.

But Sin's children decided to make a tomb for the sake of his descendants. Instead of scattering his ashes into the sea, they took them to the site where Sin's home had once stood,

Sin Chaeho
This photo was taken while Sin was in Lüshun Prison.

Lushun Prison
Sin Chaeho was held at this prison in Manchuria. Earlier, An Junggeun had also been incarcerated and executed here. This photo shows the facility today.

Tomb of Sin Chaeho
This tomb was built in 2008 because the original one kept collapsing. The new tomb lies close to its former site, at Gwirae-ri in Chungcheongbuk-do Province. The bronze statue on the left stands at Cheongju Arts Center.

in Gwirae-ri, Chungcheongbuk-do Province, and buried them.

Sin was consistent throughout his life, whether studying history or fighting for independence. He always finished what he had started: that's why I have so much respect for him.

While Sin was in prison, a string of his history books was published back in Joseon: *Joseonsa yeongu cho* ("Exploratory Studies in Korean History"), *Joseon sanggosa* ("An Early History of Korea") and *Joseon sanggo munhwasa* ("An Early Cultural History of Korea"). He also wrote novels, essays and poems. Here's one of his poems:

I am your love and you are mine.

If a sword were to slice us apart,

out would gush a lovely red stream of blood.

I would take it in my hand

and sprinkle it all across the land.

Wherever it fell,

new flowers would bloom in spring.

'Dream-Heaven' - a novel by Sin Chaeho

Sin wrote several novels, including *Kkumhaneul* ("Dream-Heaven"), *Yong-gwa yong-ui daegyeokjeon* ("A Battle Between Two Dragons") and *Ilmokdaewang-ui cheoltoe* ("The Mace of the One-eyed King").

Kkumhaneul tells the story of protagonist "The Man," who dreams one night of dying and passing into the afterlife. He meets General Eulji Mundeok, witnesses the Battle of Salsu River and fights hard against foreign invaders to save his country. The Man then goes to hell, where he meets Gang Gamchan, a lion guarding the gates. Gang tells him that traitor Yi Wanyong is inside. The Man now travels to heaven, where he encounters many of the greatest heroes in Korean history. He takes a brush and sweeps the dust from heaven, while resolving to fight and secure a clear, blue sky for the Korean nation.

Sin uses *Kkumhaneul* as an allegorical framework to talk of love for country and nation, and of the future of the independence movement.

A history of pain and blood

Park Eunsik, like Sin Chaeho, campaigned for independence by studying his nation's history. He was twenty-one years older than Sin. While the latter devoted himself to studying antiquity, the former concentrated more on contemporary history, including things he had seen and heard himself.

Park wrote two books covering the period of his own lifetime, 1864 to 1920: *Hanguk tongsa* ("The Tragic History of Korea") and *Hanguk dongnip undong-ji hyeolsa* ("The Bloody History of the Korean Independence Movement"). Writing a history of your own era is no easy task: just imagine trying to make sense of all the things going on around you today and arrange them coherently in a book. Only historians with courage and conviction can pull off such a task.

The words *tongsa* and *hyeolsa* in the titles of Park's books literally mean "pain-history" and "blood-history." The most important thing in history, he believed, was "spirit." "Even if a country has lost its independence, it can never be destroyed as long as its spirit survives," he would say. "Preserving the nation's spirit means preserving its history." Park's words are similar to those of Sin Chaeho, who claimed, "You must read history if you want to awaken the spirit of patriotism."

Like Sin, Park studied Chinese and Confucianism as a boy. When he grew up, however, he realized the need for reform and attempted to raise awareness among his fellow Koreans by writing in newspapers and magazines like the *Capital Gazette*. He was active in the Provisional Government in Shanghai, too. *Hanguk tongsa* and *Hanguk dongnip undong-*

ji hyeolsa were originally written in Chinese but have now been translated into Korean, making them much more accessible to Koreans today.

Park and Sin were both "nationalist historians," whose studies revolved around their own nation. Other Korean nationalist historians include Jeong Inbo, An Jaehong and Mun Ilpyeong.

–Independence Hall of Korea

'Hanguk tongsa' and Park Eunsik
The title of this book means "The Tragic History of Korea."

CHAPTER 9

Yi Bongchang
and Yun Bonggil

"Japan is discriminating against and abusing Koreans. ... Killing the Japanese emperor was the quickest way to bring Joseon closer to independence, so I decided to sacrifice myself while killing him for the sake of my 20 million fellow Koreans. My assassination attempt was not the work of one wanton individual, but a front-line action on behalf of the entire Korean nation, which longs for independence."

TIME LINE	1931	1932	1936
	Colonial period	**Colonial period**	**Colonial period**
	Sin Chaeho's *Joseon sanggosa* serialized in *Chosun ilbo*	Yi Bongchang and Yun Bonggil attack Japan	Sohn Keechung wins Berlin Olympic marathon

Have you ever heard of the "lunchbox bomb" incident? This assassination by patriot Yun Bonggil of several Japanese dignitaries during the colonial period is well known in Korea today. But Yun was preceded by another patriot, Yi Bongchang, who staged an even more daring attempt to strike back at Japan by throwing a bomb at the emperor himself.

Yi is far less famous in Korea today than Yun. This is because Yun's attack was successful whereas Yi's failed, and because Yun's family has done a better job of keeping his memory alive.

Despite its failure, Yi's assassination laid the path that Yun followed, and is highly significant in that it took place in Tokyo, the heart of the Japanese empire, and targeted none other than Emperor Hirohito.

Let's start with the story of Yi Bongchang's attack.

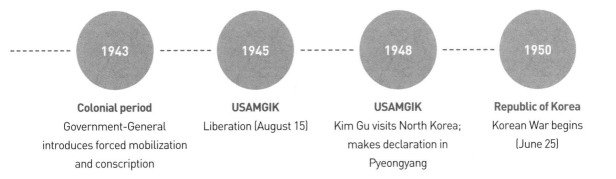

1943	1945	1948	1950
Colonial period	**USAMGIK**	**USAMGIK**	**Republic of Korea**
Government-General introduces forced mobilization and conscription	Liberation (August 15)	Kim Gu visits North Korea; makes declaration in Pyeongyang	Korean War begins (June 25)

At around 11:45 in the morning on January 8, 1932, thick crowds filled the sidewalks outside Tokyo Police Headquarters. They were waiting to catch a glimpse of Emperor Hirohito, who was due to pass by on his way from the imperial palace just ninety meters away. Yi Bongchang squeezed his way to the front of the crowd and waited for the emperor's horse-drawn carriage.

The emperor's carriage
This photo was taken just before Yi Bongchang threw his grenade.

Yi Bongchang's patriotic deed

Soon, the imperial procession drew near. Yi's heart was pounding. The first carriage held one passenger, but Yi believed it to be somebody else. He waited for the next one. Certain that this carriage bore the emperor, Yi took out the hand grenade in his pocket and hurled it at its target.

The crowd broke into screams at the loud explosion. Unbelievably, though, the carriage just kept going. All the grenade had done was make a big noise; no harm was done apart from a few scratches to the floor and wheel of the carriage and some shrapnel wounds to the horses behind. And it turned out that the emperor had been riding in the first carriage after all.

"I've failed," Yi lamented. But he soon regained his composure as he saw the Japanese policemen rushing towards him.

Yi makes his move
Yi's attack is often known as the Sakuradamon Incident, after the main gate of the imperial palace in Tokyo. In fact, Yi threw his grenade not by the palace gate but in front of Tokyo Police Headquarters, about ninety meters away.

"I'm not running away," he said. "So there's no need to be rough."

Yi was arrested and tried in a Japanese court, where he explained why he had tried to kill the emperor:

"Japan is discriminating against and abusing Koreans. I believe that Koreans must regain independence and get their own country back by any means possible. When Baek Jeongseon (another name of Kim Gu) said that killing the Japanese emperor was the quickest way to bring Joseon closer to independence, so I decided to sacrifice myself while killing him for the sake of my 20 million fellow Koreans. My assassination attempt was not the work of one wanton individual, but a front-line action on behalf of the entire Korean nation, which longs for independence."

Yi was hanged at around nine in the morning on October 10, 1932, in Ichigaya Prison. He was thirty-two years old. His actions caused an international stir, while both China and Japan found new respect for Koreans.

Outside Tokyo Police Headquarters
Japanese police inspect the scene of the assassination attempt, with Tokyo Police Headquarters in the background. Yi's grenade was acquired by Kim Gu through a Chinese contact. When it failed to cause much damage, Yi bitterly regretted not testing out a similar one first.

Down with Japan!

Before the dust had even settled after Yi's assassination attempt, another heroic deed sent shockwaves through Japan.

Yun Bonggil's bomb
Yun threw the bomb that he had hidden in his water bottle. He meant to use the one in the lunchbox, shown in this photo, to kill himself afterwards. The photo was kept as a secret document in Japan's National Diet Library, then released to the public in 2004. Below it are models of both bombs.
– The Patriot Maeheon Yun Bonggil Memorial Association

This time, the incident took place in Shanghai and the protagonist was Yun Bonggil.

April 29, 1932, around three months after Yi Bongchang's Tokyo bombing, was Tenchosetsu, a Japanese national holiday marking Emperor Hirohito's birthday. A celebration to mark the festival was held in Hongkou Park, Shanghai. Though the emperor himself was not in attendance, a lineup of high-ranking Japanese officials and military top brass had turned up.

Smartly dressed, Yun packed a lunchbox, a water bottle and

Aftermath of the attack
This photo was taken immediately after Yun's bomb went off.

a Japanese flag and made his way calmly to the park. In the lunchbox and water bottle were two bombs. Soon, the event began. Yun moved closer to the stage on which the Japanese dignitaries stood. When the Japanese national anthem started playing, he threw one of the bombs. A huge explosion rang out, and the stage was plunged into chaos.

"Down with Japan!" Yun cried out as the Japanese police rushed at him.

! 'I had a bomb, too!'

On the day Yun threw his bomb in Hongkou Park, another man had planned a similar attack. His name was Baek Jeonggi and he was a member of a South China-based Korean pro-independence group. Baek had been due to take action at ten in the morning, an hour before Yun, but for some reason the Chinese man who had arranged to buy him a ticket for the event never turned up. In the end, the appointed time passed and Yun launched his own successful attack.

Baek was later arrested after getting caught trying to attack a banquet hall where the Japanese ambassador and several soldiers were eating. He was put in prison, where he died at the age of thirty-nine. His tomb now lies next to those of Yun Bonggil and Yi Bongchang in Seoul's Hyochang Park.

Baek Jeonggi
The Korean independence association of southern China to which Baek belonged was an anarchist group, other members of which included Yi Hoeyeong, Yu Jamyeong and Jeong Hwaam.

This time, the bombing was a great success. The commander of the Japanese armed forces was taken to hospital but died after twelve operations, while the Japanese minister in China lost a leg. The commanders of the Third Fleet of the Imperial Japanese Navy and the Ninth Division, as well as the consul general, were heavily injured. Yun was incarcerated in Kanazawa military prison in Osaka, then executed by firing squad at twenty minutes before noon on December 19, 1932, at the age of twenty-five. His death came some two months after that of Yi Bongchang.

Joseon pride

Both Yi Bongchang and Yun Bonggil were members of the Korean Patriot Corps, a group founded and commanded by Kim Gu and attached to the Provisional Government in Shanghai. Kim created the corps for an important reason.

At this time, Japan had captured Manchuria and was about to take the whole of China. The Provisional Government, meanwhile, was struggling through a period of severe stagnation, prompting Kim Gu to write in his autobiography, *Baekbeom ilji* ("The Principles of Kim Gu"), "In no direction, I felt, was there a path towards preserving even the name of the Provisional Government, let alone its work." Morale in the exiled government had hit rock bottom. Kim believed some kind of special action was needed to breathe new life into his organization and get the flames of passion burning again. This was why he created the Korean Patriot Corps.

Kim Gu and the Korean Patriot Corps
Kim posed for this photo with Choe Hongsik, Yu Sanggeun and another member of the corps.

The corps's first actions were Yi and Yun's attacks, news of which electrified the people of Joseon. China began to admire the country's spirit of independence and promised to help the Provisional Government, providing just the boost it needed. Yi and Yun's actions revitalized the organization and conveyed Koreans' pride to the world.

One thing is worth considering here. You will recall the terrorist attack on New York's World Trade Center on September 11, 2001. This event shocked the world and raised the question of whether terrorism was a justifiable means, whatever its ends. Many innocent people died, after all. So couldn't the same question be applied to the action of Yi and Yun?

These two young Koreans did not kill any innocent people. Their attacks led to the deaths of high-ranking officials and military men, figures who bore responsibility for Korea's colonial occupation. Still, this raises another question: could killing the Japanese emperor or a few generals really have led to independence? In fact, Yi Bongchang himself wondered about this. Before leaving for Japan, he asked Kim Gu:

"Even if I succeed, I don't think it will lead straight to Korean independence. What will you do afterwards?"

Kim's reply was firm:

"I don't think just a couple of actions will lead straight to independence for Joseon, but if we keep repeating our attacks, I believe we can be certain of success. We're sending you as our first martyr, so please achieve your goal in a spirit of patriotism. I plan to send more men of character like you in the future, if I can find them."

Yi had strong faith in Kim's words.

A worker and a 'yangban'

Giving your life for your country is far from easy. So who were Yi Bongchang and Yun Bonggil, these men who so readily made the ultimate sacrifice?

Yi was born in 1901 in Wonhyoro, near today's Yongsan Station in Seoul. He was seven years older than Yun. His family was originally wealthy, but while he was growing up it became too poor even to send him to school. He abandoned his studies and began earning a living at the age of fifteen. Yi did whatever job he could find, working in a cake

Kim Gu and Yun Bonggil
Yun was a member of the Korean Patriot Corps, created by Kim Gu.

shop, in a pharmacy and as a laborer at the railway station.

Yi was a thoroughly unremarkable young man. When the March First Movement kicked off, he was working as a shop assistant in Japanese-run Murata Pharmacy. He had a vague notion that some kind of protest with cheering was going on, but no idea why, so he just carried on working busily.

Yi traveled to Japan in search of a better job. No matter how hard he worked, though, his nationality made him subject to discrimination and contempt. In order to escape such treatment, he masqueraded as a Japanese and found a job in a soap factory. His excellent command of the local language allowed him to pull this off. As time passed, however, Yi felt ever more acutely that this life in denial of his nationality was nothing but a sham.

Yi left Japan and made his way to Shanghai. He visited Kim Gu at the headquarters of the Provisional Government and told him of his desire to join the independence struggle. After meeting Yi several times, Kim came to trust him and decided to give him the task of assassinating Emperor Hirohito.

Before setting off again for Japan, Yi joined the Korean Patriot Corps, swore an oath, and had his photograph taken. In it, he stands in front of a Taegeukgi, a copy of the oath around his neck, a grenade in each hand, and a huge smile on his face.

'Tokyo jagan-ui jinsang' ('The True Story of the Tokyo Operation')
Kim Gu wrote this text about Yi Bongchang's attempted assassination of the Japanese emperor in Tokyo. It narrates Yi's life story and achievements in detail, and suggests that all Koreans fast on the anniversary of his execution in tribute to his sacrifice.

Yi Bongchang
Yi posed in front of the Taegeukgi for this photo before he left for Tokyo. He holds a grenade in each hand. His beaming smile makes quite an impression.

Repatriating Yun Bonggil's remains
This photo shows Yun's remains being taken back to Korea after liberation, in May, 1946. He was given a funeral, then buried in Seoul's Hyochang Park.

The oath reads as follows:

"With the utmost sincerity, I swear to become a member of the Korean Patriot Corps and slaughter the leaders of the enemy in order to restore the independence and freedom of the motherland."

Yi became aware of the need for independence while working in shops and as a laborer in Japanese-owned companies. Yun Bonggil, by contrast, was born into the Yun clan of Papyeong, a renowned *yangban* family, and entered the independence struggle from a very different background.

Yun was born in 1908 in Yesan, Chungcheongnam-do Province. After studying Chinese at the *seodang* run by his uncle, he worked as part of a rural enlightenment movement,

Tombs of the Three Martyrs
Yi Bongchang, Yun Bonggil and Baek Jeonggi are buried at this site, known as the Tombs of the Three Martyrs, in Seoul's Hyochang Park. The park was originally called Hyochangwon and contained the grave of Prince Munhyo, the son of King Jeongjo of Joseon. Munhyo's grave has now been relocated and the park is home to the Tombs of the Three Martyrs and those of Kim Gu, key members of the Provisional Government and the empty tomb of An Junggeun.

teaching illiterate peasants to read and write. While Yi Bongchang never married, Yun married Bae Yongsun at the age of fifteen and had two sons. After deciding to seek work in the wider world, he left his family in his hometown and traveled to China alone. He was twenty-three years old.

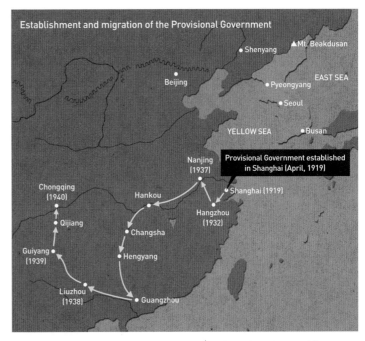

After Yi Bongchang and Yun Bonggil's patriotic deeds, the Provisional Government gradually migrated from Shanghai to Chongqing. This map shows the route it took.

In Shanghai Yun met An Gonggeun, brother of An Junggeun, who was working in the Provisional Government. An introduced Yun to Kim Gu, which was how Yun ended up joining the Korean Patriot Corps and bombing the event in Hongkou Park.

Yi and Yun's actions brought new life to the struggling Provisional Government. Kim Gu must have been extremely grateful to the two young men. He remembered them all the way to liberation, after which he set out to find their remains. As a result, Yi and Yun were finally returned to the bosom of their motherland in 1946 and reinterred in Seoul's Hyochang Park.

The Liberation Army OSS

Korean Liberation Army founding ceremony
This ceremony took place in Chongqing in 1940 and was attended by various Chinese politicians, foreign ambassadors and diplomats.

The Korean Liberation Army was attached to the Shanghai Provisional Government. Kim Gu, leader of the Provisional Government, created a special unit within the army, called the OSS. It was led by Yi Beomseok, who had won fame alongside Kim Jwajin at the Battle of Qingshanli.

Kim planned to deploy the OSS inside Joseon, to conduct advance operations. At this point, World War II was approaching its end. Japan was fighting against the United States, and Kim believed Joseon would only be recognized as a legitimate independent state if it fought alongside the US. He therefore created the Liberation Army OSS with the cooperation of America's own Office of Strategic Services.

Fifty brave young Koreans volunteered to take part in the unit's special operations, which would mean certain self-sacrifice. After three months of hard training in Xi'an, the special forces unit was ready. Detailed plans were made to deploy its members secretly into Joseon by airplane or submarine, to conduct a variety of operations. It was now August 1945.

As they waited impatiently to be sent into action, the OSS troops received an unexpected bit of news: Japan had surrendered! Kim Gu should have jumped for joy, but in fact he was bitterly disappointed that the OSS had not been able to conduct its advance operations inside Joseon. The soldiers felt the same. One of them, Kim Junyeop, later became president of Korea University. In his memoir *Jangjeong* ("A Long March"), he described his feelings at the time as follows:

"We should have whooped with joy, jumped up, kicked our chairs over and danced in jubilation. But General Yi [Beomseok] and I were in no mood for celebration. We regretted not having the chance to drive the Nips out by ourselves, and were gutted that all our plans had come to nothing."

How different would things have been if Japan had surrendered just a little later, and the advance operations planned by Kim Gu had gone ahead? Just imagine.

OSS troops and their American instructors

Kim Gu (left) and OSS head William J. Donovan (right)
Provisional Government president Kim Gu and OSS leader William J. Donovan after a meeting to discuss plans for joint operations between the Korean Liberation Army and the OSS.

CHAPTER 10

Koreans who amazed the world

Germany at this time was ruled by Hitler and the Nazis; great expense and effort had been put into the Berlin games, with the aim of demonstrating German superiority to the watching world.

More than two hours after the starting gun, the Olympic stadium began to fill with a sense of excitement. Who would be the first athlete to run in and win the race? Before long, Sohn Keechung appeared on the track.

The sight of the Korean athlete bursting to victory through the finishing tape that day remains one of the immortal scenes in sporting history.

TIME LINE

1931

Colonial period
Sin Chaeho's *Joseon sanggosa* serialized in *Chosun ilbo*

1932

Colonial period
Yi Bongchang and Yun Bonggil attack Japan

1936

Colonial period
Sohn Keechung wins Berlin Olympic marathon

Korean dance fans may be familiar with the name Choi Seunghee. A hugely popular dancer in the colonial period, she even toured the world in her heyday—something almost unheard of for a Korean artist at the time.

Many young Koreans today have never heard of Choi, largely because she went to live in North Korea after liberation. Nonetheless, she exerted huge influence on Korean dance.

There were two other stars just as famous as Choi during the colonial period: Sohn Keechung and Nam Sungyong, who won gold and bronze medals, respectively, in the marathon event at the 1936 Summer Olympics in Berlin.

Choi, Sohn and Nam amazed the world with their achievements and brought great hope and joy to the people of Joseon in an age of stifling colonial oppression.

Let's find out more about these star Koreans today.

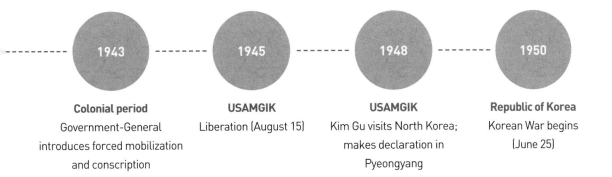

The marathon race at the Games of the XI Olympiad began in Berlin at 2:59 in the afternoon of August 9, 1936. Sohn Keechung and Nam Sungyong ran the race as part of the Japanese delegation, with Japanese flags pinned to their chests. Germany at this time was ruled by Hitler and the Nazis; great expense and effort had been put into the Berlin games, with the aim of demonstrating German superiority to the watching world.

More than two hours after the starting gun, the Olympic stadium began to fill with a sense of excitement. Who would be the first athlete to run in and win the race? Before long, Sohn appeared on the track.

The sight of the Korean athlete bursting to victory through the finishing tape that day remains one of the immortal

Sohn Keechung approaches the finish
Sohn entered the Olympic Stadium in Berlin in clear first place.
Nonetheless, he kept up the pace all the way to the finishing line.
What would have been going through his mind?

Sohn with Leni Riefenstahl
Photographer and director
Riefenstahl featured
Sohn in several scenes
of *Olympia*, the official
documentary of the Berlin
Olympics. This photo
was taken when Sohn
visited Germany in 1956.
Riefenstahl died in 2003,
aged 102.

scenes in sporting history. After running 42.095 kilometers without a break, he sprinted the final 100 meters at full pace. Once past the finishing line, he simply kept on running, a blank expression on his face. No whoop of joy, no elaborate victory celebration. He had won the race with a new world record of two hours, twenty-nine minutes and 19.2 seconds.

This scene was included in *Olympia*, the official documentary film of the Berlin Olympics. The director, German photographer Leni Riefenstahl, took a special interest in Sohn, inviting him to visit her home.

The saddest victory

Sohn's new world record had broken the two hour, thirty minute barrier. Behind him came Englishman Ernie Harper, followed by Nam Sungyong in third place. The taking of both first and third place by Asian athletes in an Olympics mostly dominated by Germany and the United States created a huge buzz in the international press.

When Sohn and Nam stepped onto the rostrum for the medal ceremony, they were met with thunderous applause by crowds filling the stadium, including Hitler himself. The two men were now living the dream of every athlete. Yet far from beaming proudly under their laurel wreath crowns, they hung their heads and looked utterly miserable. What was going on?

The flags on Sohn and Nam's chests were red Japanese suns, while the anthem filling the stadium was also that of Korea's colonial occupier. Most of those watching the ceremony naturally assumed that the two Asian athletes in front of them were Japanese. Inwardly, they longed to cry out and tell the world that they weren't, and that the flags on their chests should have been Taegeukgi. Later on, Sohn described how he felt that day in the stadium:

"Young people today don't know what it's like to lose

The Olympic medal ceremony
The sight of Sohn and Nam looking so miserable even as they wear their laurel wreath crowns is quite moving.

Nam Sungyong
This photo shows Olympic athletes returning from Berlin. Nam stands second from the front. Sohn retired after the Olympics, but Nam went on to run the 1947 Boston Marathon with eventual winner Suh Yoonbok, finishing tenth.

your country. When the Japanese national anthem started playing after I won, my head dropped. Normally, a medal-winning athlete stands proudly on the rostrum as he watches his national flag being raised. Nam Sungyong and I had to watch the Japanese flag go up and hear *Kimigayo*, the

The 'Japanese flag erasure incident'

Sohn and Nam became even more famous due to a media controversy that came in the wake of their victories. The scandal erupted when two Korean newspapers, the *Joseon jungang ilbo* ("Joseon Central Daily") and *Dong-a ilbo*, acquired video copies of the Berlin medal ceremony, captured a still photo of Sohn in his laurel wreath crown to accompany their articles on his victory, and deleted the Japanese flag on his chest before publishing it. Meanwhile, *Singajeong* ("New Family"), a magazine published by the same company as the *Dong-a ilbo*, ran a photo of Sohn's legs only, with his upper body cut out altogether, accompanied by the caption, "These are the legs of Sohn Keechung, winner of the Berlin marathon and son of the Korean nation."

Japan responded by issuing a publishing ban on the two newspapers and magazine and locking up the editors responsible.

The disappearing flag
The "Japanese flag erasure incident" got *Dong-a ilbo* sports correspondent Yi Giryong banned from reporting. Society desk chief Hyeon Jingeon, photo desk chief Sin Nakgyun, and Yi Sangbeom, the artist who deleted the image of the flag, were arrested and locked up by the police.

Japanese anthem, even though we had won victory for Korea. Words can't express the sorrow of having no country and not being able to share the joy of victory."

Despite the sad circumstances, Sohn and Nam had made a huge gift of joy and pride to the people of Joseon at a time of suffocating oppression by Japan.

Most people today only remember Sohn Keechung for his victory. But Nam Sungyong was every bit as remarkable an athlete. Both men were born in 1912, Sohn in Sinuiju, Pyeonganbuk-do Province and Nam at the other end of the country, in Suncheon, Jeollanam-do. They conquered the marathon world at the age of twenty-five and even died close together, with Nam passing away in February, 2001 and Sohn in November, 2002.

Berlin was not Joseon's first participation in the Olympic marathon. Two of its athletes had participated in the previous tournament in Los Angeles in 1932, where Kim Eunbae and Kwon Taeha finished sixth and ninth in the men's event, respectively. Since this was also during the colonial period, Kim and Kwon were part of a Japanese delegation too.

The first Korean to achieve global marathon victory under his own flag was Suh Yoonbok, who won the Boston Marathon in

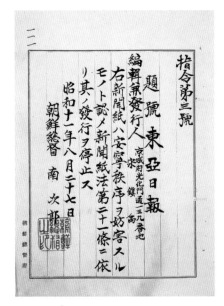

Publication of the 'Dong-a ilbo' is suspended
This order from the Government-General suspended publication of the *Dong-a ilbo* on the grounds that it had obstructed social stability and order.
–Independence Hall of Korea

Helmet awarded to Sohn Keechung
This bronze ancient Greek helmet was given to Sohn for his victory in the Olympic marathon. Sohn himself only received it fifty years later, in 1986. It was the first foreign item to be registered as an official "Treasure" by the Korean government and has now been donated to the National Museum of Korea.

Suh Yoonbok
Suh crosses the finishing line to victory in the Boston Marathon on April 10, 1947.

1947, two years after liberation. In 1950, Ham Keeyong, Song Giryun and Choe Yunchil surprised the world by taking the top three places, respectively, in the same event. And Hwang Youngcho won the men's race at the 1992 Summer Olympics in Barcelona.

Sohn stopped running marathons after returning to Joseon. He entered Bosung College (now Korea University), then went to study in Japan. After liberation he remained active in the world of sports; later, as an old man, he made the following reflection:

"Life is a marathon with no half-way point. And there's no turning back, so you have to always do your best if you want to reach the finish line with no regrets."

Choi Seunghee, 'danceuse coréenne'

In late 1938, two years after Sohn and Nam's thrilling marathon victory, dancer Choi Seunghee gave a performance in Paris. In the program, she was described not as Japanese but as a "danceuse coréenne" ("Korean dancer").

The performance was a great success, met with rapturous applause by artists such as Pablo Picasso, poet Jean Cocteau and novelist Romain Rolland. Following her France performance, Choi continued to Belgium, Italy, the

Netherlands and Switzerland, drawing admiration in each country. Europe's critics showered her with praise, calling her the "international dancer of the Orient."

Choi was born in Seoul and attended Sookmyung Girls' Middle and High School. In her student days, she proved to be a talented musician. Around the time of her graduation, she went with her brother to watch a performance by Japanese contemporary dancer Ishii Baku; it was then that she decided to follow a career in dance rather than music. She followed Baku to Tokyo to study under him.

Returning to Joseon three years later, Choi founded a dance institute in Seoul's Jeokseon-dong neighborhood. Around this time, she met and married a young man named An Pilseung who had studied Russian Literature at Waseda University in Japan and was active in KAPF (Korea Artista Proletaria Federatio), a group of Koreans in the arts.

Interference by the colonial authorities extended to the world of arts at the time. When members of KAPF were rounded up on charges of opposing Japan, An ended up in prison.

With An still behind bars, Choi toured provincial Korea. As well as performing, she created new dances; most of her works at this time referred to the pain of her

Choi Seunghee
This image dates from the 1930s.

Performance program
Upon returning from her world tour, Choi became known in Korea as the "international dancer."

Choi Seunghee and family
This photo shows Choi with her husband and daughter, Seonghui. After going to live in North Korea with her mother, Seonghui grew up to become a dancer too.

incarcerated husband or contained criticism of Japan.

When An was released, Choi went with him and their daughter, Seungja (who later changed her name to Seonghui) to Japan to meet Baku. Her plan was to continue studying. Around this time, she discovered Korean dance. Choi realized that her works so far had had little to do with her own national traditions, and resolved to create dances with a uniquely Korean character.

She now turned her attention to the wider world, in the belief that her duty was to make Korea's dance talent internationally known. An became her manager and worked hard to support her. He also changed his name to An Mak.

In 1938, Choi and An traveled to the US, where Choi performed in Los Angeles and New York. They then carried on to France, where their smash-hit tour of Europe began. Next, the couple headed back across the Atlantic to Latin America, giving performances in Brazil, Uruguay, Argentina, Peru, Chile, Colombia and Mexico.

Choi gained a reputation as "one of the world's top ten dancers." Returning to Joseon four years and some 140 international performances later, she had truly become a Korean global star.

Collaborator or communist?

In 1943, Choi traveled to China to give morale-boosting performances to Japanese troops. Many Koreans angrily branded her a collaborator for dancing in front of the enemy and donating money to the Japanese war effort. Later, one of the musicians who performed with her recalled what had gone on:

"Each night, after Choi Seunghee had danced for the Japanese troops, her husband would appear, take the money and disappear somewhere. After a while, I found out he was donating it to the independence armies."

Is this true? Was Choi pretending to be close to the Japanese army but secretly supporting her own country?

When Joseon was liberated, Choi was in China. But liberation was soon followed by national division, with the country cut in half along the thirty-eighth parallel. Soviet troops entered the northern section of the peninsula and Americans the south. At this point, Koreans based in China, Russia and Japan during the colonial period were forced to

Choi teaches students at the Central Academy of Drama in Beijing

Choi and members of her dance troupe in North Korea
Was Choi Seunghee a pro-Japanese collaborator? Or a communist, since she went to North Korea after liberation? This mystery remains unsolved.

Choi Seunghee
and Sohn Keechung
This photographer managed to capture the two
biggest stars of the time in a single shot.

choose whether to return to the north or the south of their divided homeland. An Mak chose North Korea. Choi returned to the South with her son Byeonggeon and daughter Seonghui, her brother-in-law An Jeseung, and his wife Kim Baekbong. Later on, she went to join her husband in the North.

In North Korea, Choi formed a new dance troupe and achieved several dazzling successes. Her dance drama *Joseon-ui eomeoni* ("The Mother of Joseon") won first prize at The Third World Festival of Youth and Students in Berlin in 1951, and she received the title *inmin baeu* ("people's actress"), one of North Korea's highest artistic accolades. This period did not last long, however: from around 1967, she was forced to abandon her career after being banned by the North Korean authorities on charges of failing to create the kind of dance demanded by their leaders.

Meanwhile, in South Korea, the very mention of Choi's name was taboo for many years because of her move to the North. Recently, however, a television program was broadcast in the South to mark the ninetieth anniversary of her birth. Her dance style survives here to this day thanks to her student, Kim Baekbong, who came to the South during the Korean War.

Kim Yeom, Film Emperor of Shanghai

In 1932, Shanghai film magazine *Diansheng* ("Movietone") held a poll to pick the "Emperor of Film." The winner was a Korean actor named Kim Yeom, who took first place in three categories: "Most Handsome Actor," "Actor I'd Most Like to Be My Friend" and "Most Popular Actor." Born as Kim Deoknin, he chose the name Yeom, which means "flame," or "blaze," after resolving to become an actor and live his life in a blaze of glory.

How did a Korean end up as China's emperor of film? Kim first emigrated from Joseon at the age of two, when his father moved to China as part of the independence movement. After his father died, Kim went to live with the family of

Kim Yeom in 'Yecao xianhua'
Kim's films were extremely popular in mainland China, making him the pride of ethnic Koreans living there. So why is he so unknown in Korea today? Probably because he remained in China after Korean liberation, dying in Shanghai in 1983 at the age of seventy-four.

his aunt and her husband, Kim Gyusik. During his lonely teenage years, he dreamed of becoming a film star.

Unlike today, film acting was looked down upon as a profession for those of disreputable backgrounds. Nonetheless, Kim believed he could achieve great things as an actor. Against the wishes of his family, he held onto his dream.

Kim took on various odd jobs in Shanghai, selling film tickets and cleaning movie theaters. In the mean time, he worked hard to become an actor.

Film, particularly the latest Hollywood fare, was wildly popular in Shanghai at this time. After a few years, Kim finally got noticed for his role in a film called "*Yecao xianhua*" ("Wild Flower Among the Weeds"). This was followed by a series of hits such as "*Ye meigui*" ("Wild Rose") and "*Dalu*" ("The Big Road"). Kim's films drove young Chinese wild, and they would often imitate his gestures and manner of speaking. He came to symbolize the figure of a young man yearning for a new society. Even the Japanese spotted him and asked him to appear in their own films, but Kim flatly refused.

CHAPTER 11

Stolen youth, rotten minds

Meanwhile, at Bansei Airbase in Kagoshima, Kyushu, the tangled bodies of 47 Koreans were discovered under a single pine tree.

No one knows for sure just how many Koreans died like this, or in how many similar places, since Japan has destroyed all records. But the number is certainly high, as suggested by the rumor was that one Korean died for every sleeper on the railways they laid.

Colonial period

Sin Chaeho's *Joseon sanggosa* serialized in *Chosun ilbo*

Colonial period

Yi Bongchang and Yun Bonggil attack Japan

Colonial period

Sohn Keechung wins Berlin Olympic marathon

The book, Terezin: Voices from the Holocaust *is a collection of books and writing by Jewish children who died in a German concentration camp during World War II. Its contents convey the sheer cruelty of Nazi Germany's treatment of Jewish prisoners. Nowadays, many books and films about this terrible chapter in history have gained it global notoriety.*

But when it comes to Japan's atrocities against Koreans, which were every bit as cruel as those of Germany, even many Koreans are unaware of just what went on. The aspiring empire also abducted countless Korean women to serve its troops as wartime sex slaves. Some people are in favor of covering up these episodes from the past, considering them shameful. What's the use of digging up something you can't change anyway, they say.

I think that's wrong: you can't plan for the future without reflecting thoroughly on the past. If we simply cover things up, what's to stop them happening again? And shouldn't we keep ourselves aware of the agony of war so that we never underestimate the value of peace?

That's why I'm going to tell you about the tragedy and pain that our ancestors suffered.

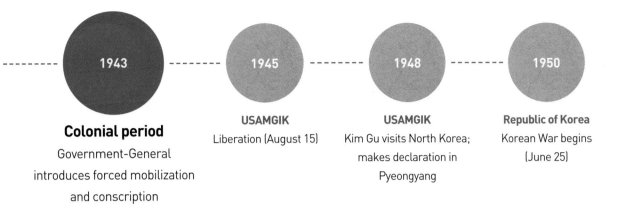

1943

Colonial period
Government-General
introduces forced mobilization
and conscription

1945

USAMGIK
Liberation (August 15)

1948

USAMGIK
Kim Gu visits North Korea;
makes declaration in
Pyeongyang

1950

Republic of Korea
Korean War begins
(June 25)

A few years before liberation, Japan launched itself into World War II, fighting against the United States across Asia and the Pacific region. As part of this massive war effort, it forcibly mobilized Koreans to build its airfields and other military installations and to work in its coal mines.

Those drafted this way had to endure backbreaking hard labor in harsh conditions. Here, I'll tell you a story about workers at Bibai Coal Mine in Hokkaido.

World War II
As its name suggests, this war was fought on a global scale between the Allies, including the US, Britain, France and the Soviet Union, and the Axis, led by Germany, Italy and Japan. Germany and Italy were led by Hitler and Mussolini, respectively; their Asian counterpart was Emperor Hirohito of Japan.

Korean workers massacred

"All they fed us was salt broth and a bowl of rice with beans. We had to work barefoot as we had no shoes. We would get up at four in the morning, work in the mine all day, then return to our living quarters at seven or eight, when the manager would lock our rooms from the outside. We couldn't go out whenever we wanted. They called it living quarters, but it was effectively a prison.

Once there was an explosion in the mine and more than 100 people died. 80 of them were Korean, including about 10 from my team. Many people tried running away when they couldn't take it any more. If they caught you trying to escape, they would flog you to death. I also thought about running away. After all, what was the difference between dying at the mine and getting killed for trying to escape? If I was going to die anyway, I thought it might as well be while I was trying to run away."

Mine workers died in accidents, floggings after attempted

Koreans slaughtered en masse
Sometimes, Koreans drafted to work on the construction of airbases and other military installations were put to death in order to maintain secrecy.

escapes, or from disease.

To make matters worse, the Japanese did not hesitate to kill all the workers drafted for a project once it was finished, in the name of secrecy.

In November 1944, as the end of the war approached, Japan began building a huge underground military facility in Matsushiro, Nagano. A few thousand Koreans were among the workers drafted for the project. They worked under the supervision of Japanese military police.

One day, when construction was almost finished, several hundred Koreans suddenly disappeared. All of them had been working on a particular part of the bunker complex. A rumor started to spread: the missing Koreans had been killed in order to prevent military secrets being leaked. Meanwhile, at Bansei Airbase in Kagoshima, Kyushu, the tangled bodies of 47 Koreans were discovered under a single pine tree.

No one knows for sure just how many Koreans died like this, or in how many similar places, since Japan has destroyed all records. But the number is certainly high, as suggested by the rumor was that one Korean died for every sleeper on the railways they laid.

Young Koreans sent into battle

As World War II approached its end, Japan began sending

Medical examinations for conscripts

A Korean conscript
Young Koreans were put in Japanese uniforms and sent to fight with the Japanese military against the US. At the time, the two powers were fighting each other in the Pacific region. This photo shows twenty-year-old Korean Yun Taebong at his home on the morning of August 15, 1945, just before he left for battle. A few hours later, Japan announced its surrender and Yun was able to avoid going to war.

Korean youth and students to fight. Signing up was voluntary at first, but was later replaced by mandatory conscription. Many university students found themselves drafted, put in uniform and dodging bullets on the front line practically overnight.

That wasn't all. In 1944, Japan passed a law ordering the formation of special units of female workers. The decree forced girls and women between the ages of twelve and forty to join "labor initiative units" and work in factories to produce the goods needed for the war effort. These are often known in Korean as *jeongsindae*, roughly meaning "initiative units." Though frequently equated with so-called comfort women, the workers in initiative units were different. It's wrong to use the terms interchangeably.

Initiative unit workers labored in factories, while

comfort women were young Koreans, between the ages of fifteen and nineteen, forced to go to the front line and serve as sex slaves for Japanese troops. The latter had been drafted since the 1930s, long before the labor initiative unit decree was promulgated.

Comfort women
These women look exhausted and barely able to sit upright. After liberation, they were offered no comfort or compensation. Instead, they were forced to struggle with poverty and disease while covering up their histories.

Comfort women were sent anywhere where Japanese troops were fighting: Manchuria, other parts of China, the Philippines, Okinawa, Hokkaido and elsewhere. When Japan lost the war, it disposed of its used sex slaves by driving them into caves and throwing in bombs, massacring them in trenches, or even putting them all on a ship and deliberately sailing it into a mine to kill them all. When they didn't even have time for this, the Japanese sometimes simply abandoned the women, leaving them wandering around foreign countries while trying to scrape a living.

Those who returned to Korea lived by concealing their pasts. It didn't occur to the South Korean government to look after them. Finally, in 1991, an elderly former comfort woman named Kim Haksun found the courage to come forward and testify about her experience, whereupon the issue received worldwide attention. The UN, too, issued an official statement declaring that the mobilization of comfort women had contravened international law. Japan, however, continues to

'Kkeullyeogam' ('Dragged Away')
This painting is by elderly former comfort woman Kim Sundeok. Until her death in 2004, Kim lived with other former comfort women at a home called House of Sharing in Toechon, Gyeonggi-do Province.

deny all responsibility. Many former comfort women remain overseas, unable to return home. How many Koreans were dragged off to work in factories, coal mines and war zones, or as comfort women? Since, as I've just said, Japan has destroyed its records, we'll never know the precise figures. But we can make estimates.

'Wednesday Protest' outside the Japanese embassy
Since January 1991, former comfort women have gathered every Wednesday at noon to demonstrate outside the Japanese embassy in Jongno-gu District, Seoul.

Collaborators transformed into great men

While many Koreans were being sent to their deaths as military conscripts or comfort women, others were gaining themselves money and success by collaborating with Japan.

We often associate the term collaborator with figures such as Yi Wanyong and other four Eulsa Traitors who approved the Protectorate Treaty and Japan's annexation of Korea. But there were plenty of other collaborators, too.

When I first heard exactly who had collaborated with Japan, I was amazed. Many of them were famous people I had learned about at school or read about in biographies, where they were portrayed as heroes.

Historian Choe Namseon, author of the March First Movement declaration of independence; Choe Rin, one of the people's representatives; Yi Kwangsu, the famous novelist— these were the people who filled my school textbooks, the people whose texts I had dutifully underlined and memorized for my exams. If they were collaborators, how come they had been portrayed as great men and assigned such important roles in my education?

This strange phenomenon is due to a lack of reflection on the past. The wrongdoings of pro-Japanese collaborators were not properly criticized or reflected upon but simply overlooked, leaving them free to depict themselves as

Korea's losses
Between the beginning of World War II in 1939 and liberation in 1945, 4.5-4.8 million Koreans were mobilized, 1.2-1.5 million forcibly relocated to Japan, 300,000-400,000 taken to China or Southeast Asia, and 100,000-130,000 drafted as comfort women: roughly 7 million people altogether. The total population of Joseon at the time was 22-24 million, meaning that a third of all Koreans were forcibly mobilized, in one way or another, by Japan.

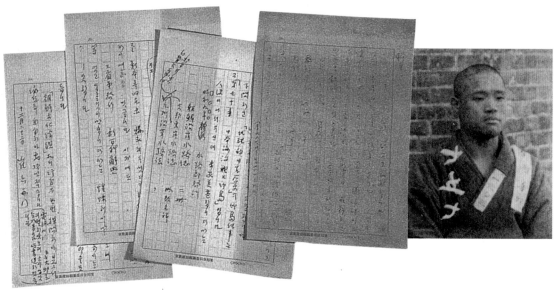

Choe Namseon and handwritten manuscripts
Choe was arrested and imprisoned for drafting the Declaration of Independence used during the March First Movement. This photo of him was taken in Seodaemun Prison. After his release, he was active as a historian but collaborated with Japan on many occasions.

Yi Kwangsu's 'Minjok gaejoron'
Yi Kwangsu was the author of *Mujeong* ("The Heartless"), one of Korea's most important early novels. In May, 1922, he published an essay titled *Minjok gaejoron* ("Treatise on National Reconstruction") in the magazine *Gaebyeok* ("Genesis"). The piece calls for a reconstruction of the Korean national character itself, based on the argument that it is lazy, selfish and inferior, and therefore incapable of achieving independence. These claims are identical to those used by Japan to justify its invasion of Joseon.

independence fighters after liberation.

France spent years under German control during World War II. There, by contrast, Germany's stooges were exhaustively identified, criticized and made to express remorse after liberation.

Let's see what some of Korea's leading collaborators got up to in the colonial period.

"By now, I have developed the following conviction: Koreans must forget everything about being Korean. Their blood, their flesh, even their bones, must become Japanese."

So wrote Yi Kwangsu in the *Maeil sinmun* ("Daily News") in 1940. Yi was Korea's most famous author at the time; every word he wrote was tremendously influential. After embarking on a pro-Japanese path with the essay *Minjok gaejoron* ("Treatise on National Reconstruction"), Yi was one of the first Koreans to comply with the colonial policy of replacing Korean names with Japanese ones, rebranding himself "Kayama Mitsuro."

Koreans queue up for Japanese names
These people are waiting to change their Korean names to Japanese ones as demanded by the colonial authorities. The order was implemented as part of the Ordinance on Civil Matters in Korea of 1939.

While young Koreans of both sexes were being dragged off to fight Japan's war, many pro-Japanese collaborators gave speeches encouraging them to go. Choe Namseon, historian and author of the famous independence declaration issued on March 1, 1919, was one such figure.

"What can this be called if not a war of justice, a holy war?" he said. "I urge every last one of you to join the battle."

Helen Kim (Kim Hwallan), then principal of Ewha College (now Ewha Womans University), also praised the war in a text titled *Jingbyeongje-wa yeoseong-ui gago* ("Conscription and the Resolve of a Woman"). Kim adopted the Japanese name "Yamagi Katsuran."

Some Korean newspapers and magazines also collaborated with Japan's agenda, running articles in support of colonial rule, praising the war and supporting forced mobilization, or encouraging conscription and special units.

Japan put forward the *naisen ittai* doctrine, which held

The Oath of Imperial Subjects (children's version)
• We are subjects of the Greater Japanese Empire.
• Together, we stand devoted to His Majesty the Emperor.
• We will grow tougher through endurance to become fine, strong citizens.

that Japanese and Koreans were "of the same body," and an "imperialization" policy whereby Koreans were considered subjects of the Japanese emperor. It forced Koreans to speak only Japanese, to memorize the "Oath of Imperial Subjects," to take Japanese names, and to worship at Shinto shrines. This was not an attempt to genuinely afford Koreans equal status to Japanese, but to mobilize them for Japan's war

Anxious to live a whole life untainted by shame

While Yi Kwangsu and other leading novelists and poets sang Japan's praises, one man wrote poems that felt like candles to light the darkness. His name was Yun Dongju and he was a student at Yonhee College (today's Yonsei University). This is the prefatory poem to his anthology *Haneul-gwa baram-gwa byeol-gwa si* ("Sky, Wind, Stars and Poetry")

Anxious to live a whole life untainted by shame,
I find myself tormented even by the wind in the trees.
I must love all things mortal, just as I sing of the stars in the sky.
I must walk the path I've been given.
Tonight, too, the wind brushes past the stars.

Yun was imprisoned on charges of being an independence activist and died on February 16, 1945, just six months before Joseon's liberation.

Yun Dongju
This photo shows Yun as a student at Yonhee College (now Yonsei University). He is buried in Longjing in Manchuria, where he spent his childhood.

effort.

Japan made all Koreans in schools and government offices recite the Oath of Imperial Subjects every morning. There were two versions, one for adults and one for children. Amazingly, the oath was drafted not by a Japanese

Worshipping at a Shinto shrine
Japan's policy of "imperializing" Koreans included compulsory worship at Shinto shrines. This policy held that Koreans were also subjects of the Japanese emperor.

but by a Korean named Kim Daeu. When liberation came, Kim is said to have sobbed in grief at Japan's defeat.

What on earth were these collaborators thinking as they acted as Japan's stooges? Some of them were foolish enough to be deceived by Japanese propaganda, while others were not taken in but still believed firmly in Japan and its agenda. Still others collaborated with their colonial occupier simply to further their own success and prosperity, despite knowing that its propaganda was all lies.

Investigating Korea's collaborators

Newly-liberated Joseon's first task was to punish pro-Japanese collaborators. The National Assembly passed the Special Act for the Punishment of Anti-Nation Activities and created the Special Committee for Investigation of Anti-Nation Activities.

The special committee had arrested those who had been high-ranking officials under the colonial regime, those who had persecuted independence activists and their families, abusive policemen, those who had spied for Japan, those who had collaborated with the Japanese war effort by running military factories making airplanes and ammunition, and those who had written texts supporting Japan's aggression.

The first man the special committee detained was Park Hongsik, chairman of the conglomerate Hwashin and owner of a company that manufactured airplanes. Park was arrested first to stop him fleeing the country. Next was Lee Jonghyeong, who had played a leading role in helping the Japanese army hunt down Korean independence fighters in Manchuria. Some of the many others detained by the committee included No Deoksul, a policeman notorious for torturing independence activists; Kim Daeu, author of the Oath of Imperial Subjects; Bae Jeongja, Ito Hirobumi's adoptive daughter; novelist Yi Kwangsu; March First Movement popular representative-turned-pro-Japanese collaborator Choe

Arrestees of the Special Committee
Many of those investigated or arrested by the Special Committee for Investigation of Anti-Nation Activities later became lawmakers and officials. Others were active in educational and cultural spheres.

Rin; and historian Choe Namseon. In total, the committee had around 680 people arrested or earmarked for arrest.

The general public welcomed the special committee's activities. These collaborators had flourished while many other Koreans died; now, they were getting what they deserved.

Sadly, the special committee was disbanded after less than a year. All those it had had arrested were released and the Special Act for the Punishment of Anti-Nation Activities came to nothing. Why?

Even after liberation, many South Korean politicians had ties to former collaborators. Judging that it was not in their interest to have these figures punished, they grew increasingly vociferous in their opposition to the Special Act and branded its proponents communists.

Yun Deogyeong's villa
Yun was the uncle of Empress Sunjeonghyo, Sunjong's wife. He was given the title "viscount" by the Japanese after the annexation. Yun prospered by collaborating with Japan.

"This law promotes national disunity," they said. "It's the work of communists in the National Assembly."

"All those calling for punishment of collaborators are commies."

Even President Syngman Rhee disapproved of the Special Committee. Eventually, it was abolished and the issue of collaboration swept aside.

As I've already said, most pro-Japanese collaborators were well-known public figures. Now, they were able to hold on to their prominent positions while concealing their track records of collaboration. This is how their names and writings kept appearing in South Korean school textbooks.

The issue of punishing pro-Japanese collaborators clearly illustrates how failure to come to terms with the past can lead to a twisted future.

CHAPTER 12

Liberation and national division

After thirty-five years of hardship under oppressive colonial rule, the news of liberation seemed like a dream. They now hoped to rebuild their long-lost country and live in freedom and happiness.

Sadly, their hopes were soon dashed. As I mentioned earlier, the Korean Peninsula immediately became embroiled in a conflict of interests between the great powers.

The road from the Daehan Empire through the colonial period was littered with tragic events. The years of colonial rule, of course, were darkest of all. From here onwards, we'll be exploring Korean history from liberation to the present. When liberation came, the people of Joseon dreamed of a free and happy future. But this wasn't to be the case: Japan's exit was soon followed by the division of the peninsula into northern and southern halves.

Many Koreans remember the special edition of the TV program National Singing Contest *that was filmed in Pyeongyang. This long-running South Korean show, broadcast by KBS, showed ordinary Koreans singing their favorite songs. Each episode was filmed in a different part of the country—only in the South, of course. But in August, 2003, a very special edition showed a joint North-South singing contest that took place in Pyeongyang's Moran Park. Many Korean children watching the show were too young to understand the complexities of national division, but their curiosity was stoked by extraordinary pictures being beamed from another country—or was it?—full of Koreans that looked just like them and sang in the same language. Who or what had cut Korea in half? Was it that thing called the "communist party?" Korea was divided in highly complicated circumstances. Perhaps the principal reasons were that it was caught in the middle of a conflict between global powers, and that it proved incapable of escaping their influence.*

Today, let's take a closer look at how national division occurred.

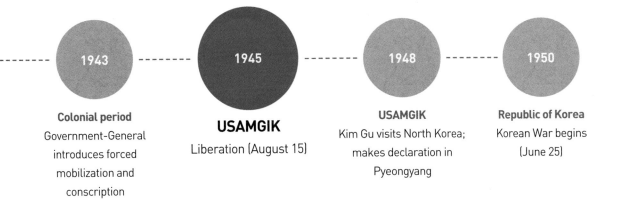

1943	1945	1948	1950
Colonial period	**USAMGIK**	**USAMGIK**	**Republic of Korea**
Government-General introduces forced mobilization and conscription	Liberation (August 15)	Kim Gu visits North Korea; makes declaration in Pyeongyang	Korean War begins (June 25)

At about eight in the morning on August 6, 1945, a silver B29 bomber appeared in the sky above the Japanese city of Hiroshima. Anyone looking up at that moment might have seen a small object fall from its underbelly. Some fifty seconds later, a blinding wave of heat and light engulfed the city. A mushroom cloud rose high into the sky. For the first time in history, an atomic bomb had been used, reducing Hiroshima to ashes and killing everyone within 500 meters of ground zero in an instant.

Three days later, on August 9, the Americans dropped another nuclear bomb, this time on the city of Nagasaki. The day before this, on August 8, the

Japanese in Seoul
Japanese living in Seoul listen to a radio broadcast of Emperor Hirohito announcing their country's surrender at noon on August 15, 1945.

Japan surrenders
Japanese's representative signs the Instrument of Surrender on board USS Missouri, which was anchored in Tokyo Bay at the time.

Liberation
Korean crowds cheer ecstatically at being freed from Japanese rule.

Soviet Union had declared war on Japan. Finally, the self-styled Empire of the Sun could hold out no longer. It announced that it would accept the terms of the Potsdam Declaration, which demanded its unconditional surrender.

At noon on August 15, 1945, the thin, trembling voice of Japanese emperor Hirohito addressed his subjects in a live radio broadcast:

"After pondering deeply the general trends of the world and the actual conditions obtaining in our empire today, we have decided to effect a settlement of the present situation by resorting to an extraordinary measure.

We have ordered our government to communicate to the governments of the United States, Great Britain, China and the Soviet Union that our empire accepts the provisions of their joint declaration."

Japan's surrender meant liberation for Joseon, whose people ran into the streets in celebration. After thirty-five years of hardship under oppressive colonial rule, the news of liberation seemed like a dream. They now hoped to rebuild their long-lost country and live in freedom and happiness.

Sadly, their hopes were soon dashed. As I mentioned earlier, the Korean Peninsula immediately became embroiled in a conflict of interests between the great powers.

The fateful thirty-eighth parallel

Did the US really need to use atomic bombs? By August 1945, Japan was already showing signs of considering a surrender. Fellow Axis powers Italy and Germany had already capitulated, leaving it to face the Allies alone—a fight it was bound to lose. America chose to use its fearsome new weapon both to accelerate Japan's surrender and to display its overwhelming power, even once the war was over, to the

US troops enter Seoul
Koreans warmly welcomed the American troops as they arrived, believing them to have liberated the country. But the US had other ideas: it planned to occupy and rule Joseon, even intending to leave the Japanese former governor-general in charge.

The Taegeukgi rises on Mt. Namsan
After liberation, the Japanese flag at the summit of Mt. Namsan was replaced by a Taegeukgi.

whole world.

As soon as Japan declared an end to hostilities, the US and the Soviet made each other a promise: they would divide the Korean Peninsula along the thirty-eighth parallel, with Soviet troops occupying the northern half and American troops the south.

The United States was the first to suggest taking the thirty-eighth parallel north as a line of division. The Soviet Union was in a position to occupy much more of the peninsula, but agreed to the American proposal because its leaders were more interested in Manchuria than Korea. This unassuming feature on a map now became the fateful line that divided an entire nation, and continues to do so to this day.

In August, 1945, Soviet troops entered the Korean Peninsula ahead of their American counterparts. Led by Lieutenant General Ivan Chistyakov, they stayed north of the thirty-eighth parallel as agreed. Later, on September 8, US troops landed in southern Korea. The two superpowers set up military governments to administer their respective halves of the peninsula.

Long-awaited independence had arrived, but the Soviet and US militaries had divided Korea and were now ruling it themselves.

For the next three years, the people of Korea endured

suffering no less than that of the colonial period itself. Once the great powers had cloven the peninsula in half, conflict between North and South grew ever greater. The former, under Soviet influence, followed a path of socialism, while the latter gravitated towards American-style capitalism. The two Koreas were now moving in completely different directions.

I'll die with you.

The atomic bombs dropped on Hiroshima and Nagasaki took several million lives, including those of many Koreans living in the two cities. Even those that survived were often tormented by strange, radiation-related sickness for the rest of their lives. In many cases, these illnesses were passed on to their offspring. Yi Jeongja, who was caught in one of the atomic blasts at the age of fifteen, retained symptoms of breathlessness into adulthood. Her children, too, suffered from various ailments. "None of my children are in normal health. ... Sweat flows from my youngest daughter's armpits all year round ... It frightens me when she turns quiet. That's when she asks me why

Hiroshima Peace Memorial
This dome was left in a state of destruction following the bombing of Hiroshima in order to remind future generations of the horror of atomic bombs.

I gave birth to her, and those are the words I hate and fear above all else. When I can't find an answer, she tells me resolutely, 'When you die, I'll die with you'."
Unfortunately, the victims of the atom bombs and their descendants have yet to receive any compensation from either the South Korean or the Japanese government.

What were we doing?

While foreign military governments appeared in the northern and southern halves of their country, what were Koreans themselves doing? Had they been completely unprepared for liberation? As you know, they had sustained various independence movements throughout three-and-a-half decades of colonial rule.

Immediately before liberation, preparations had begun for the building of an independent nation in the event of Japan's surrender. Independence campaigners still inside Joseon had formed the Committee for the Preparation of Korean Independence (CPKI), led by Lyuh Woonhyung, and were getting ready for liberation.

The day after the surrender was announced, some 5,000 people gathered at Hwimun Middle School in Seoul to hear an address by Lyuh.

"The day of liberation for the Korean nation has arrived. ... Now that we have taken our first steps into freedom, we must forget the pain and bitterness of the past and build a rational, ideal paradise in this land. ... We must march ever forward, in unison and solidarity."

The CPKI was full of hope for its new nation-building project. But things turned out not to be easy. The US military government was neither very aware of sacrifices

The Committee for the Preparation of Korean Independence
The CPKI was formed on August 15, 1945, to prepare for the building of a new nation. Its chairman was Lyuh Woonhyung. Regional committees were formed across the country, all with the same aim.

and aspirations of the Koreans who had fought so long for their independence, nor particularly interested. It made no attempt to acknowledge even the Shanghai Provisional Government itself, let alone any of the other independence groups that had

Lyuh Woonhyung after his speech
This image shows Lyuh after delivering his speech on August 16, the day after liberation, at Hwimun Middle School in Seoul. Lyuh had been an independence activist in the colonial period. After liberation, he worked to build a new Korean state until his assassination in 1947.

fought in and outside Korea, or the preparations made by the CPKI to rebuild the country. The Americans were quite explicit about this, proclaiming that their military government, commonly known as USAMGIK (United States Army Military Government in Korea), was "the only government south of the thirty-eighth parallel."

USAMGIK's top priority was making Korea south of the thirty-eighth parallel work to the advantage of America rather than the Soviet Union. Korean independence, nation-building and everything else came second.

The divisive issue of Trusteeship

In late December, 1945, four months after liberation, the foreign ministers of the US, Britain and the Soviet Union met in Moscow to discuss the fate of the Korean Peninsula. There, the United States proposed placing Korea under

The Yalta Conference
This summit meeting
was held by US president
Roosevelt, British prime
minister Churchill and Soviet
premier Stalin in Yalta,
Ukraine, in February, 1945,
shortly before liberation. The
three leaders agreed on a
trusteeship arrangement for
Joseon rather than granting
it independence straight
away in the event of Japan's
defeat. The suggestion
originally came from the
American side.

the "trusteeship" of four powers—America, Britain, China and the Soviet Union—for five years. This term denoted an arrangement whereby Korea would be administered by the four foreign states. The Soviet Union responded by suggesting the establishment of a provisional government instead.

America had never planned to grant Korea independence from the start. Several years earlier, then-president Roosevelt had proposed a trusteeship period of twenty to thirty years. Doubtful that this colony was able to rule itself, he claimed that such an arrangement was needed until it acquired the capacity for independence. This pretext sounded plausible enough, but the US's actual intention was to make sure the Korean Peninsula remained within its field of influence. At the time, Stalin had agreed to Roosevelt's proposal. The shorter the trusteeship period the better, the Soviet leader had added.

The great powers were not interested in how long the people of Joseon had waited for independence, or how hard they had fought for thirty-five years to attain it. Their greatest concern was extending their own spheres of influence as far as possible.

The Moscow talks ended in an agreement on the establishment of a provisional government, an outcome closer to the Soviet side's original suggestion. The powers would further discuss trusteeship once the new provisional government was in place. Somehow, the *Dong-a ilbo* managed to blurt out the news from Moscow in a large headline that missed the mark in almost every way:

Anti-trusteeship demonstration
When a Korean newspaper reported that the US, Britain and the Soviet Union had decided at the Moscow conference to place Korea under trusteeship, furious protests broke out across the country. This image shows mounted policemen breaking up one such demonstration.

"USSR Calls for Trusteeship; US Advocates Immediate Independence; Soviets Support Division along 38th Parallel and Occupation"

This piece of misreporting not only attributed the call for trusteeship to the Soviet Union, rather than the US, but mistakenly claimed that the Moscow talks had settled on trusteeship instead of a provisional government.

Nonetheless, the headline sent shockwaves through Joseon. Its people longed above all for independence, and were outraged at the suggestion of trusteeship. There was widespread fury at the Soviet Union for its alleged stance.

A few days later, news of the Moscow conference reached Joseon in its correct form. But by then it was too late: Koreans already firmly associated the talks with trusteeship and believed it to be the Soviet position.

Anti-trusteeship movements arose across the country. Those who opposed it were considered patriots; those in favor were traitors. Before long, the issue had thoroughly polarized Korean society.

Trusteeship divided Koreans into advocates of the Soviet Union on one hand and those of the United States on the other. Or, to put it another way, supporters of socialism and of capitalism, respectively. Before liberation, the nation itself had been the most import measure of political ideology; now, the foremost question was that of who was socialist and who was capitalist. Former pro-Japanese collaborators now quickly became passionate capitalists and looked for ways to get ahead again.

The conflict between left- and right-wingers grew deeper as time went by. Effectively, this equated to the conflict between northern and southern Korea, since each side of the thirty-eighth parallel was controlled by the Soviet Union and the US, respectively.

Socialism and capitalism remained in fierce conflict for some fifty years after World War II. Known as the Cold War due to its nature as a prolonged, tense stand-off that seldom erupted into armed conflict, this global struggle was headed by two superpowers: the Soviet Union on one side and the United States on the other. Though they had fought on the same side as recently as World War II, the two states were now fierce rivals and showed no sign of their previous amity. Korea's national division, too, was a product of the Cold War.

The Berlin Wall
This Wall, which had divided Germany, fell on November 9, 1989. Delighted Germans climbed on top of it and cheered through the night.

Still, perhaps the great powers would have had a harder time cutting the country in half if its people had united instead of splitting along ideological lines. If only they had managed to do so...

Two other countries shared Korea's fate in the aftermath of World War II: Germany was divided into eastern and western states, and Vietnam into northern and southern halves. In both cases, the splits left socialists on one side of the border and capitalists on the other. Now, however, both Germany and Vietnam are unified states again, while reunification remains Korea's biggest task.

What is socialism?

Socialism first reached Korea in the Japanese colonial period, as part of an influx of various new foreign ideologies. But were socialism and communism the same thing? At first, socialism was the only word going around. People first began talking of communism some time during World War I. So you could say socialism was the word used up until World War I, and was later replaced by communism. But people tend to use them interchangeably anyway.

Socialism is an ideology developed by German philosopher Karl Marx. Its aim is to bring about an equal society. Marx was inspired to look for a bold new alternative as he witnessed the misery of workers in the early days of capitalism, during Europe's Industrial Revolution.

People often talk about democracy as the opposite to socialism, but its true antithesis is capitalism. So what does that make the opposite of democracy? The answer is dictatorship, or totalitarianism, as exemplified by Nazi Germany or imperial Japan during the colonial period.

Socialism and capitalism only oppose each other along economic lines, whereas the difference between democracy and dictatorship or totalitarianism is political. Which means democracy is compatible with both socialism and capitalism.

The first country to try and put socialism into practice was the Soviet

Park Honyong
The Korean Communist Party was formed under Park's leadership in 1925. The Japanese authorities were strong suppressors of socialism; the party collapsed following the arrest of its leaders and was later re-formed. This process was repeated several times. After liberation, Park went to North Korea, where he became deputy prime minister but was executed after the Korean War on charges of spying for the US. This photo was included with a letter he sent in 1946, immediately after liberation, to his daughter, Viviana, whom he had placed in an orphanage in Moscow. She later became a dancer.

Union, led by Russia. It was followed by several Eastern European states, India, China, North Korea and others. But the Soviet Union disintegrated in 1990, while various Eastern European states began abandoning socialism in favor of capitalism. North Korea remains socialist today, following its own brand of the ideology under the home-made label of the "Juche Idea."

When socialism reached Korea during the colonial period, many independence activists embraced it as a means of achieving national liberation and autonomy. Many others were interested in the ideology, too, if not active supporters. This was due partly to curiosity and partly to attraction to the equality for which socialism aims. In any case, it's clear that those who espoused socialism in the colonial period had independence and liberation as their goals. These people carried on their socialist campaigns after liberation and became known as left-wingers.

Questions of left and right crop up frequently in most accounts of Korean history since the war. Left-wingers are often referred to using words like communists or reds. In fact, the terms left-wing and right-wing originally had nothing to do with communism or socialism but appeared in revolutionary France in the late-eighteenth century. After the revolution, members of the National Assembly divided into three groups, with moderate Girondins to the right of the president, radical Jacobins to the left, and the centrist Plain party in the middle, whence the terms right-wing, left-wing and centrist.

CHAPTER 13

Kim Gu crosses the thirty-eighth parallel

Kim Gu readily agreed to cross the thirty-eight parallel and visit the north. Many people tried to talk him out of it, some out of concern for his safety, and some because they suspected he was a communist. But Kim stuck to his decision.

"Even if the thirty-eighth parallel cuts me in half, I must spare the nation the same fate," he said firmly.

TIME LINE ---------

1931

--------- -------

1932

-------- -------

1936

Colonial period
Sin Chaeho's *Joseon sanggosa* serialized in *Chosun ilbo*

Colonial period
Yi Bongchang and Yun Bonggil attack Japan

Colonial period
Sohn Keechung wins Berlin Olympic marathon

Every Korean has heard of Kim Gu. Even today, many politicians name him as one of their heroes. He was just as popular after liberation, when his record as head of the Provisional Government made him one of Joseon's most respected independence activists.

One day, a crowd of people gathered outside Kim's house, Gyeonggojang. They had heard rumors that he planned to travel into North Korea, across the thirty-eighth parallel, and wanted to stop him. Soon, Kim appeared on the second-floor balcony. "I'm going to North Korea on behalf of the nation, so don't try and stop me!" he roared. What did this most popular of independence leaders plan to do in the North? Let's find out.

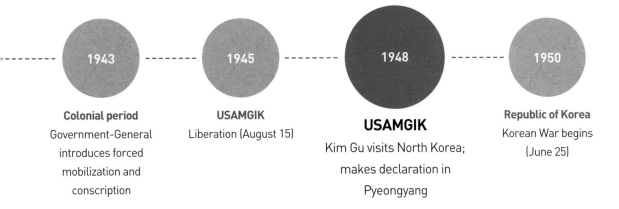

1943

Colonial period
Government-General
introduces forced
mobilization and
conscription

1945

USAMGIK
Liberation (August 15)

1948

USAMGIK

Kim Gu visits North Korea;
makes declaration in
Pyeongyang

1950

Republic of Korea
Korean War begins
(June 25)

Three years after liberation, Koreans had still not managed to set up an independent state. Their country remained divided. Couldn't they just have got on with holding elections, creating a national assembly, and setting up a government headed by an elected president or prime minister? For some reason, none of these tasks was proving easy to achieve.

Suddenly, it was announced that elections would be held and a government set up south of the thirty-eighth parallel only. Most Koreans were bewildered. Why hold elections in the South while excluding the North? What did this mean for the future of the country?

Kim Gu fiercely opposed holding elections only in the South, as this would lead to permanent national division.

May 10 Election poster
The May 10 election was the first in Korea after liberation. It was held only in the south.
–National Folk Museum of Korea

Syngman Rhee and his supporters, on the other hand, supported the plan.

Unilateral elections in the south

The decision to hold elections only south of the thirty-eighth parallel was fundamentally due to conflict between the US and the Soviet Union, the world's two superpowers. I'll do my best to explain this, but it's still a complicated story so I hope you won't have too much trouble following.

Now that the Cold War had begun, Korea was emerging as its biggest area of contention. The Soviet and American armies faced off directly at the thirty-eighth parallel. The nation's journey towards independence had been hijacked by the global ideological conflict and come to a halt.

While relations between the US and USSR gradually deteriorated, the conflict between the halves of Korea that they ruled respectively grew worse too. Each superpower wanted a solution to the Korean problem that worked in its favor and placed the entire peninsula within its sphere of influence.

When the decisions taken at the Moscow conference were

not properly implemented, the US referred the Korean problem to the United Nations. Its high degree of influence in the UN at this time led it to believe that the latter would reach a favorable conclusion on its behalf.

The UN General Assembly resolved to create a UN Temporary Commission on Korea, which would supervise a general election for both the north and south with seats accorded in proportion to the respective populations of each. The Soviet Union responded by calling for the establishment of an autonomous provisional government after the withdrawal of both its troops and those of the US, while denying members of the Temporary Commission access to the peninsula north of the thirty-eighth parallel.

The UN
The United Nations was established on October 24, 1945, with the aim of preventing further conflict and achieving world peace and cooperation in the aftermath of World War II. Both South and North Korea are now members of the UN.

Welcoming the UN Temporary Commission on Korea
The Temporary Commission was created by the UN to help determine the future of the Korean Peninsula. Kim Gu demanded that it allow the establishment of an autonomous, unified Korean government through elections in both the north and the south. But the commission was not allowed to operate throughout Korea as it had intended.

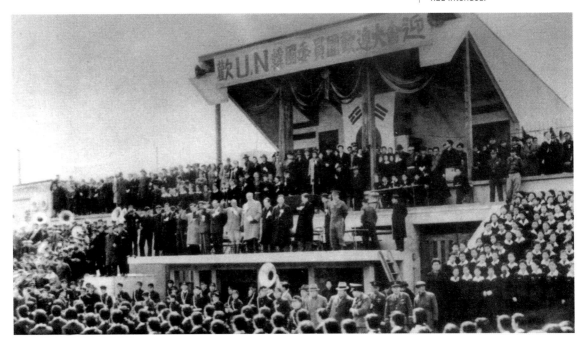

The US now proposed unilateral elections south of the boundary line to the UN. This was approved in February, 1948, by an Interim Committee of the UN General Assembly, with the election date set for May 10 of the same year. And that's how the election came to be held only south of the thirty-eighth parallel.

Kim Gu crosses the thirty-eighth parallel

Kim Gu did everything he could to oppose holding elections only in the South, including issuing a statement titled "Samcheonman dongpo-ege eupgoham" ("A Tearful Announcement to My 30 Million Fellow Koreans"):

"I will never cooperate with the establishment of a government for the south alone, even if I get sliced in half by the thirty-eighth parallel while trying to build a unified motherland. ... My 30 million Korean brothers and sisters! This is as much as I can write, for I am blinded now by tears of bitterness. I beg you to consider my predicament carefully and think hard about the future of our country."

Kim resolved to hold talks with politicians in the north. He sent them a letter via Britain and the Soviet Union.

Kim Gu speaks before heading north
Before visiting North Korea, Kim spoke to the crowd gathered outside his house. He passionately urged them to let him go, as his journey was for the sake of the nation.

"Let us discuss plans for establishing a unified government and building a new nation state through negotiations between political leaders in the north and the south. To this end, I intend to first call a conference of patriotic party leaders in the south who are in favor of north-south negotiations, in order to elect representatives. ..."

About a month later, a reply arrived from the north: "Let's hold a meeting of representatives of all northern and southern social groups that oppose unilateral elections in the south, on April 14 in Pyeongyang."

Kim readily agreed to cross the thirty-eighth parallel and visit the north. Many people tried to talk him out of it, some out of concern for his safety, and some because they suspected he was a communist. But Kim stuck to his decision.

"Even if the thirty-eighth parallel cuts me in half, I must spare the nation the same fate," he said firmly.

Kim finally crossed into the north on April 19, 1948. Upon arrival in Pyeongyang, he issued another statement:

"The thirty-eighth parallel will always exist. But the boundary drawn along it by foreign armies to divide our motherland must be completely and utterly erased. This line deprives us of unification,

Kim Gu crosses into the north
Kim crossed the thirty-eighth parallel with his secretary, Seonu Jin (left) and his son, Kim Sin. What must they have been thinking as they crossed over? They were soon followed by Kim Gyusik, the leader of a joint left-right movement to form a democratic government of unity. Kim Gyusik was also the uncle of Chinese film legend Kim Yeom.

Going to the polls
Held in 1948, the May 10
Election was the first of its
kind in Korea. How must
people have felt as they
voted for the first time?
This little boy certainly
seems to have found it
fascinating.

independence, autonomy and our nation.
And not only that. It has caused widespread
starvation, separated families, and sparked
fratricidal conflict."

Kim's delegation met Kim Ilsung and other
leading North Korean politicians, held a
conference and passed several resolutions: to
have the US and Soviet militaries withdraw
from each half of the peninsula simultaneously; to create
a unified parliament through democratic elections in the
whole country, have it pass a constitution and form a unified,
democratic government; and to reject the result of a unilateral
election in the south, even if it went ahead, on the grounds
that it did not represent the opinions of the nation.

Kim returned to Seoul on May 5, in one piece. He
demanded that US forces withdraw, while campaigning for a
boycott of the unilateral election. Nonetheless, it went ahead
as planned on May 10. It has since become known as the "May
10 Election."

This led to the inauguration of the "Republic of Korea"
in the south on August 15, 1945, with Syngman Rhee as
its president. The north responded almost immediately by
establishing the "Democratic People's Republic of Korea" on
September 9. North and South were now two completely
separate states.

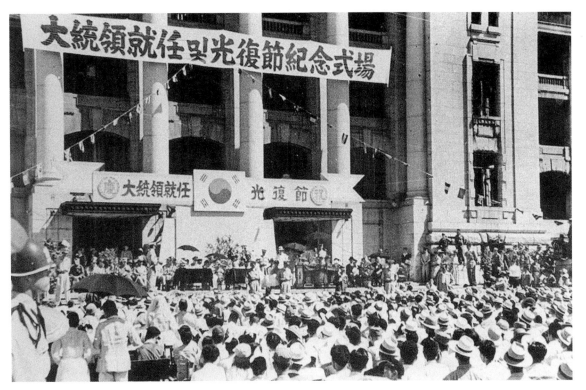

South Korea's first president is inaugurated Syngman Rhee was sworn in at this ceremony on July 24, 1948.

Two men, two paths: Kim Gu and Syngman Rhee

While Kim Gu visited the north in a bid to jointly oppose the unilateral May 10 Election in the south, Syngman Rhee played a leading role in it and ended up as president of the new state. Both men were famous former independence activists: Rhee had spent the colonial period in Hawaii, Kim in Shanghai. So why did they follow such different paths after liberation?

Kim was born in 1876 in the village of Teotgol in Haeju, Hwanghae-do Province. His birth name was Kim Changam. As a young man, he fought in a peasant army as part of the

Syngman Rhee in America
Rhee, on the far left, was
thirty years old when this
photo was taken in 1904.

Donghak Peasant Revolution. When Empress Myeongseong was assassinated, something happened that would change Kim's life forever. At a ferry port called Chihapo, he saw a Japanese man disguised as a Korean and, certain that this was one of the assassins who had murdered the queen, killed him. Kim was arrested, tried and sentenced to death, but had his sentence commuted by a special pardon from Gojong. In the mean time, he managed to break out of jail and went into hiding at Magoksa Temple, where he spent some living as a monk. Next, Kim joined a pro-independence group. He traveled to Shanghai, became the head of the group's police bureau, and eventually rose to the position of president.

Syngman Rhee, born in Pyeongsan, Hwanghae-do Province in 1875, was a year older than Kim. While the latter was fighting in a peasant army, the former was studying at Pai Chai HakDang, a new type of school, learning English from foreign missionaries and taking part in an enlightenment campaign as a member of the Independence Club. When Kim Gu was in prison for murder, Rhee was also behind bars. Kim escaped and fled to a temple, but Rhee was released with the help of missionaries and

Kim Gu delivers a speech
Here, Kim speaks
during the north-south
negotiations held at
Moranbong Theatre in
Pyeongyang on April 22,
1948.

traveled to the US.

In America, Rhee absorbed himself in study, receiving a doctorate from Princeton University in 1910. He then moved to Hawaii and made a living by contributing articles to newspapers and magazines and giving lectures. Rhee believed that independence could be achieved through diplomacy, not by armed struggle or murdering Japanese. In particular, he emphasized the importance of diplomatic ties with the US.

After liberation, both men returned to Joseon and into highly complex circumstances. Under military rule by the US and the Soviet Union, Joseon's independence activists had failed to unite, splintering instead into myriad factions. Kim commented on this situation in a speech to mark the publication of his autobiography, *Baekbeom ilji*:

"Neither Washington nor Moscow can become our capital. And nor should they. Anyone who thinks they should is no different to those who wanted Tokyo to be our capital before liberation. Seoul is our only capital. We must find, establish and assert our own philosophy."

Joseon had to find its own balance, Kim claimed, and build a new state without trusting the US or the Soviet Union. Meanwhile, on June 3, 1946, while in Jeong-eup, Jeollabuk-do Province, Syngman Rhee came out with the following

Syngman Rhee and Kim Gu shake hands
This image shows Rhee and Kim meeting at Gyeongbokgung Palace after liberation. From then on, they took different paths. Kim tried to keep Korea unified but was eventually assassinated. Rhee became the first president of half of the divided nation. How did their lives end up so different?

Kim Gu's funeral
Kim's pen name was "Baekbeom." He devised it by combining the *baek* of *baekjeong*, the butchers that constituted Joseon's lowest social class, and the *beom* of *pyeongbeomhada*, meaning "ordinary," to indicate that independence could only be achieved with the patriotic spirit of ordinary people. Perhaps that's why so many ordinary Koreans turned out for his state funeral.

comment:

"Even on its own, the south must create some kind of temporary government or committee and drive the USSR out from above the thirty-eighth parallel."

Rhee was prepared to hold unilateral elections and set up a government for the south alone. He made this argument even before the US had voiced any official support for such an election.

Why did Rhee say this? Because unlike Kim, who believed it necessary to negotiate with leaders in the north in order to prevent national division, he was unwilling to deal with the northerners even if this meant allowing the formation of two states.

Even after separate governments had been established in the north and the south, Kim refused to abandon hope and continued his struggle for unification. On June 26, 1949, he was murdered in his home at Gyeonggojang by An Duhui, a second lieutenant in the ROK Army. It is still not known who ordered the hit, however.

An kept the details of his co-conspirators a secret all the way up to his death, in October, 1996, at the hands of a fellow Korean who considered him an enemy of the people.

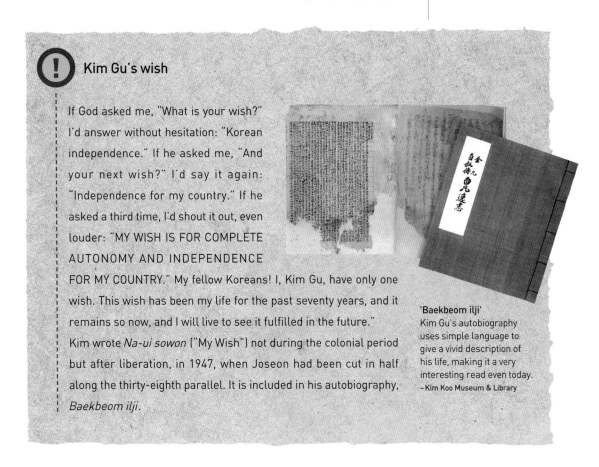

! Kim Gu's wish

If God asked me, "What is your wish?" I'd answer without hesitation: "Korean independence." If he asked me, "And your next wish?" I'd say it again: "Independence for my country." If he asked a third time, I'd shout it out, even louder: "MY WISH IS FOR COMPLETE AUTONOMY AND INDEPENDENCE FOR MY COUNTRY." My fellow Koreans! I, Kim Gu, have only one wish. This wish has been my life for the past seventy years, and it remains so now, and I will live to see it fulfilled in the future."

Kim wrote *Na-ui sowon* ("My Wish") not during the colonial period but after liberation, in 1947, when Joseon had been cut in half along the thirty-eighth parallel. It is included in his autobiography, *Baekbeom ilji*.

'Baekbeom ilji'
Kim Gu's autobiography uses simple language to give a vivid description of his life, making it a very interesting read even today.
– Kim Koo Museum & Library

The Jeju Uprising

As the May 10 Election approached, protests against the unilateral South Korean vote broke out across the country. The Jeju Uprising began as one of these. It started on April 3, with about a month to go to the election and before Kim Gu had made his visit to North Korea.

"Out with the US army now!" the crowds shouted. "Stop the unilateral election that will ruin our country!"

When election day came, voting only took place—barely—in one of the three constituencies on the island. But that was just the beginning of the affair. Once the government of the Republic of Korea had been formed and Syngman Rhee inaugurated as its president, the army was deployed to Jeju on a huge search-and-destroy mission aimed at punishing communist party members. The operation became one of indiscriminate slaughter, with many innocent islanders, adults and children alike, dying at the hands of the government troops. Two thirds of all villages on the island were burned to the ground. One of those who barely managed to survive gave the following testimony:

"They sat the women and men down in separate groups, then started spraying us with gunfire. ... A bullet went into my armpit and came out of my breast. When I came around later, I was lying among a pile of dead bodies, with my baby still in my arms. ... When they poured oil over the bodies and set fire to them there was a lot of loud crackling. You couldn't identify any remains after that."

Why on earth did this happen? How did opposing the unilateral election make the islanders communist party members? The Jeju Uprising is a tragic episode in Korean history, for which answers have yet to be provided. The people of Jeju-do still bear the emotional scars of that spring in 1948.

Memorial stone to the disappeared at April 3rd Peace Park, Jeju
This memorial stone bears the names of those who died during the Jeju Uprising but whose remains have never been found. About 3,500 names are carved on it.

CHAPTER 14

War divides a nation

North and South Korea are technically engaged in a ceasefire. In other words, the Korean War is not formally over and there is no knowing when fighting might suddenly resume.
What will it take to reach a proper peace agreement?

| TIME LINE | | 1931 | | 1932 | | 1936 | |

Colonial period
Sin Chaeho's *Joseon sanggosa*
serialized in *Chosun ilbo*

Colonial period
Yi Bongchang and Yun
Bonggil attack Japan

Colonial period
Sohn Keechung wins Berlin
Olympic marathon

One of my favorite fairy tales is called Mongsil. *I love the way it captures the atmosphere of post-liberation Korea, and tells a story similar to what one of my distant relatives went through. The eponymous heroine spends the Korean War looking after Nannam, her little step-sister. Her father has died from wounds sustained on the battlefield, while her stepmother has starved to death after giving birth to Nannam. The war wasn't just about soldiers in combat. Millions of children fought desperate battles of their own against hunger and the pain of losing their parents.*

Mongsil sees a North Korean soldier in her village.

"Who's worse, the Korean People's Army or the ROK Army?" she asks her. "Why are they killing each other?"

I wonder just the same thing. Why did the KPA and the ROK Army fight each other? The Korean War was a conflict between North and South Korea, but also one between America and the Soviet Union, and between capitalism and socialism. Some scholars even call it a proxy war, conducted in Korea on behalf of the US and USSR when they should have been doing their own fighting. Let's see how it started and, three years later, how it finished.

1943
Colonial period
Government-General introduces forced mobilization and conscription

1945
USAMGIK
Liberation (August 15)

1948
USAMGIK
Kim Gu visits North Korea; makes declaration in Pyeongyang

1950
Republic of Korea
Korean War begins (June 25)

The Korean War broke out two years after separate governments were established in northern and southern Korea. As the Cold War between America and the Soviet Union escalated, North-South relations grew steadily worse until they reached breaking point.

At dawn on Sunday, June 25, 1950, the artillery guns of the Korean People's Army burst into life. Its tanks rumbled over the thirty-eighth parallel, heading south. North Korean troops pushed down in five directions: towards Gaeseong, Uijeongbu, Chuncheon, Gangneung and the Ongjin Peninsula.

As frantic battles were fought up by

The ceasefire line
North and South Korea are technically engaged in a ceasefire. In other words, the Korean War is not formally over and there is no knowing when fighting might suddenly resume. What will it take to reach a proper peace agreement?

the thirty-eighth parallel, the people of Seoul, barely an hour's drive to the south, went about their everyday lives as normal. They only realized what was happening at around eleven that morning, when extra newspaper editions were rushed off the press: a war was in progress.

They still weren't particularly flustered, though. There were frequent skirmishes between the two armies near the border in those days, and Seoulites assumed that this was just the latest one. Moreover, many of them firmly believed their government when it bragged that the ROK Army was far stronger than the KPA and could brush off any attempted invasion by the latter.

Seoul falls in three days

The reality, however, was completely different. Even when the KPA had swept past Uijeongbu and was on its way to Seoul, defense minister Sin Seongmo kept on claiming that the South's army was putting up a good fight.

"The ROK Army's defense of Seoul is rock solid," he claimed. "You can rest assured that we'll occupy Pyeongyang within three to five days."

Even as he made these claims, Sin secretly advised Syngman Rhee to flee the capital, which he did at three in the morning on June 27. Not even the chairman of the National

The gathering clouds of war
In late 1948, the Soviet Union withdrew its forces from North Korea. When America pulled out its own troops in June of the following year, in accordance with the decision of the UN, North Korea began preparing for war. Calls for unification by invading the North also grew stronger in the South. Syngman Rhee's government, keen to push into the north, defeat the communists and unite the country, demanded weapons and aid from the US. It was confident that it could take Pyeongyang in just three days.

Assembly was aware that the he had left. The same evening, a recorded message from Rhee was broadcast on the radio:

"The United States will help us, so do not worry," he said. "Victory will soon be ours."

The severed Hangang Bridge
Koreans fleeing south were horrified to see that the only bridge over the Hangang River had been destroyed.

In the mean time, the KPA had crested Miarigogae, a hill on the way into northeastern Seoul. At last, Seoulites realized that their government had been lying to them and hurriedly began fleeing. The northern bank of the Hangang River thronged with refugees desperately trying to get across— though there are twenty bridges over the river now, there was only one at the time.

At half-past two in the morning of June 28, a huge explosion rang out and the Hangang Bridge collapsed. The several hundred people who had been crossing it were dragged down with the crumbling structure into the river below. The ROK Army had deliberately blown it up. No matter how great the strategic need to take out the bridge, such a callous attitude toward human life was unacceptable. And weren't these people only fleeing Seoul so late because they had earlier believed their government's claims that there was nothing to worry about? The bombing of the Hangang Bridge is often criticized as the most irresponsible and inhumane act by the

South Korean government in the entire war.

The Seoulites left stranded on the northern bank had no choice but to await the arrival of the KPA. Three hours later, at five in the morning, the North's army began its attack on the city; by around half-past eleven it had completely occupied it. Three days had passed since North Korean men and tanks poured over the thirty-eighth parallel and began their all-out attack. For now, they halted their advance and waited in Seoul.

UN participation and the Incheon landing

When news broke of war on the Korean Peninsula, the US called an urgent meeting of the UN Security Council to discuss creating a UN force and deploying it in Korea. India opposed the idea, fearing it would escalate the conflict, but the resolution was passed nonetheless. The United Nations Command (UNC) was created, with US general Douglas MacArthur as its commander-in-chief. UNC comprised troops from sixteen countries, including the US, Britain and France.

But the fact that US troops accounted for ninety-eight percent of its air power, 83.3 percent of its naval forces and eighty-eight percent of its army meant that the UNC was effectively the US fighting in the guise of the UN.

While the Security Council was meeting, the KPA had crossed the Hangang River and was continuing its surge down the peninsula.

MacArthur directs the landing at Incheon
UNC commander Douglas MacArthur is the central figure holding binoculars.

Two months after the war began, it had captured all but the region of the Nakdonggang River, in Gyeongsangbuk-do and Gyeongsangnam-do provinces. Syngman Rhee urgently handed over strategic command of the ROK Army to the US military.

The combined South Korean and UN forces fought tooth and nail, taking the Nakdonggang as their last line of defense. If they allowed Daegu in Gyeongsangbuk-do and Busan in Gyeongsangnam-do to fall, the entire peninsula would be in the hands of the KPA.

After losing Seoul, the Rhee administration made Busan its temporary capital. The quiet southeastern port city suddenly thronged with desperate refugees, happy to find shelter in even the crudest of wooden shacks. They began settling into tough new daily lives.

On September 15, UNC commander MacArthur caught the KPA off-guard by launching an amphibious landing at

China joins the war
Once the newly established People's Republic of China waded into the conflict, a third world war began to look like a real possibility. This would certainly be the case if the Soviet Union also decided to join in. When MacArthur's calls for a nuclear attack on Manchuria caused widespread consternation, US president Truman now decided to replace him as UNC commander with General Matthew Ridgway in the hope of bringing a swift end to the war.

Incheon. By September 28, UN and ROK forces had retaken Seoul and the Taegeukgi was hoisted atop the government building in Gwanghwamun. They drove on, past the thirty-eighth parallel into North Korea and all the way up to the border with China at the Amnokgang River.

Feeling threatened by the UN and ROK forces on its doorstep, China joined the war. It, too, was now a socialist state like the Soviet Union and North Korea. This prompted MacArthur to call for an attack on Manchuria, in Chinese territory, using atomic bombs. In an interview later on, the now-retired general expressed regret at not having been able to implement this plan:

"I would have dropped between 30 and 50 atomic bombs ... strung across the neck of Manchuria. ... [Then, I would have] spread behind us—from the Sea of Japan to the Yellow Sea— a belt of radioactive cobalt ... it has an active life of between 60 and 120 years."

If MacArthur had had his way, the Yellow Sea and East Sea would still be heavily contaminated with radiation and the Korean Peninsula itself an uninhabitable wasteland.

Divided families

Once Chinese troops entered the war,

War orphans
Children always suffer the most in times of conflict. The Korean War produced some 100,000 orphans.

the UN and ROK forces began retreating again. A large number of North Korean citizens followed them south, anxious to escape the constant aerial bombardment and rumored nuclear attacks, or prompted by advice from the US military to flee.

North Korean ports such as Heungnam and Wonsan brimmed with refugees desperate to escape the north by sea. Countless people were separated from their children, husbands, wives and parents in the confusion—

Clambering across the Daedonggang River
After China joined the Korean War, ROK and UN forces withdrew from Pyeongyang on December 5. This photo shows refugees desperately climbing across a damaged railway bridge over the city's Daedonggang River as they flee southward.

in many cases, they would never have the chance to meet again. The war tore apart families, couples and friendships. Even today, many divided families have no idea if their lost relatives in the North or the South are even alive.

On January 4, Seoul fell once again to the KPA as UN and ROK forces continued their southward retreat. This episode is now known as the "January Fourth Withdrawal." Around a month later, however, Seoul changed hands for a fourth time. From then on, the front line hovered around the thirty-eighth parallel as the fierce fighting continued. Against this

Drawing the ceasefire line
Negotiators at Panmunjom had to agree on a ceasefire line as part of the armistice agreement. Here, US colonel James C. Murray and Chinese colonel Zhang Chunshan sign their initials on a map showing the line.

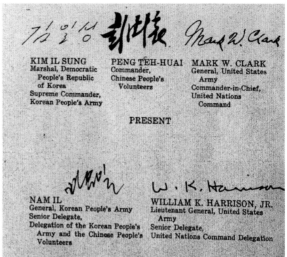

KIM IL SUNG
Marshal, Democratic People's Republic of Korea Supreme Commander, Korean People's Army

PENG TEH-HUAI
Commander, Chinese People's Volunteers

MARK W. CLARK
General, United States Army Commander-in-Chief, United Nations Command

PRESENT

NAM IL
General, Korean People's Army Senior Delegate, Delegation of the Korean People's Army and the Chinese People's Volunteers

WILLIAM K. HARRISON, JR.
Lieutenant General, United States Army Senior Delegate, United Nations Command Delegation

The Armistice Agreement
The armistice was signed by US Army lieutenant general Harrison representing the UNC and North Korean general Nam Il representing the KPA. No representative of South Korea signed the agreement.

background, ceasefire negotiations began.

The armistice talks continued for two years. In the mean time, the war rumbled on as each side fought to gain every last possible acre of territory before the conflict ended and the border was redrawn.

America's aerial bombardment of the North grew even heavier; Wonsan was bombed for a whole 861 days. Major General Oliver P. Smith of the US Navy later recalled how the bombing of the eastern coastal city was so incessant that even walking down the street there was impossible, and that going to sleep at any time of day or night would have been tantamount to suicide.

Finally, on July 27, 1953, the Korean Armistice Agreement

was signed by Lieutenant General William Harrison, Jr. representing the UNC and General Nam Il representing the KPA. Three years of war had come to an end.

The scars of war

Once the Armistice Agreement was signed, representatives of South and North Korea, China, the Soviet Union, the United States and fourteen other countries met in Geneva to discuss a peaceful solution to the situation on the Korean Peninsula. The talks ended with no clear conclusion. Ever since then, the two Koreas have remained technically at war, in a tense and prolonged ceasefire. The threat of a resumption in hostilities is ever present. This horrible state of affairs prompts many to call for a full peace agreement to replace the armistice deal— I have to say, I agree with them.

The war left both North and South Korea devastated. The latter suffered around 1 million casualties; in the former, the

Divided families
In addition to widespread death and material losses, the war left deep scars on both Koreas. Some of those who became separated from family members are still searching for them today, sixty years on.

corresponding figure was some three times higher. Railways and roads across the peninsula lay in tatters; factories and

! Memories of a North Korean POW

Jo Yunha, a native of Jeongju in Pyeonganbuk-do Province, was twenty-six when the Korean War broke out. He had never picked up a gun in his life. One day, while going for what he thought was just a medical examination, Jo suddenly found himself recruited into the Korean People's Army and ended up pushing all the way down to the Nakdonggang River.

Geoje POW Camp
This camp held North Korean and Chinese prisoners during the war. It is now a historic park.

After narrowly escaping death several times as the KPA retreated back up the peninsula, Jo was captured. He was sent to the POW camp on Geoje-do Island, off the south coast of Korea, then spent the next two years being shuffled through four more camps. Once the armistice agreement was signed, the process of releasing prisoners began. Each was asked where he or she wanted to be sent: "We had to have what they called a screening interview," he recalled. "They put us in a barbed wire enclosure, then called us one at a time. They asked us: 'Do you want to go to the North, or to stay here?' The ones that chose the North went one way, the ones that chose to stay went the other…"

Jo elected to stay in the South rather than return to his hometown. KPA prisoners who chose the South, like him, were known as "anti-communist POWs." After his release, he worked hard to adapt to life in the unfamiliar South. Anti-communist POWs were another painful legacy of the war.

buildings had been reduced to ashes.

The war also left some 200,000 women widowed and 100,000 children orphaned. Around 300,000 South Koreans were now in the North, and between 500,000 and 1 million Northerners in the South. Areas that changed hands multiple times in the war had been decimated by ideological murders in the name of communism or capitalism, and by the cycles of revenge killings that followed.

By the time the guns fell silent, North-South relations had sunk to almost irretrievable depths. They now regarded each other as sworn enemies, which was perhaps the ugliest single scar left by the conflict.

The Korean War had extensive global repercussions, too. Recession-hit Japan and the US had profited enormously from the sale of weapons, medical supplies and food devoured by the conflict. Japan earned itself 1.3 billion dollars, emerging as an economic powerhouse in the process. The war also helped galvanize the international standoff between capitalism and communism.

The SOFA and the death of two schoolgirls

In the summer of 2002, while host country South Korea was gripped by World Cup fever, a terrible incident took place in the countryside not far from Seoul. Two middle school students, Sin Hyosun and Sim Miseon, were run over and killed by a US Army armored vehicle-launched bridge as they walked along a highway in Yangju, Gyeonggi-do Province. The American soldiers involved went

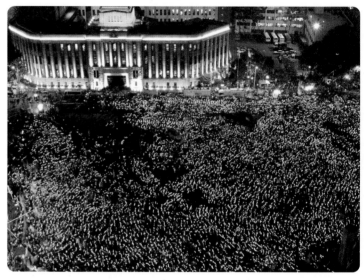

Candlelight vigil for Hyosun and Miseon
Huge crowds turned out at this vigil. The incident triggered a campaign to have the SOFA revised.

free after being tried and found not guilty. When you consider that even civilian drivers are punished for making mistakes, letting these men off the hook for killing two pedestrians seems quite incomprehensible. It was possible because of an international deal known as the US-ROK Status of Forces Agreement (SOFA). The many US troops that have remained stationed in South Korea since the end of the war are subject to the terms of the SOFA, which contains various rules and ordinances regarding their legal status on Korean soil.

The SOFA was signed in 1966 and came into force the following year. Its terms and conditions are such that US military personnel committing crimes in Korea can effectively not be tried in Korean courts. Over the years, many American servicemen caught breaking the law on Korean soil have evaded punishment due to the unequal terms of the agreement. What can be done about this? Some say the SOFA must be amended; others contend that this is unnecessary, if not impossible. The agreement is based on the premise that the Korean Peninsula is in a state of ceasefire. If this were replaced by a genuine peace treaty between North and South, surely the SOFA would no longer be needed?

Memorial stone for Sin Hyosun and Sim Miseon, Yangju-si
- The Encyclopedia of Yangju City

CHAPTER 15

Rapid growth:
a time of miracles
and tragedies

Jeon Taeil's final plea not to let his death be in vain galvanized workers across the country. They began forming unions, fighting for better conditions and defending their own rights. Jeon's death had served as a national wake-up call.

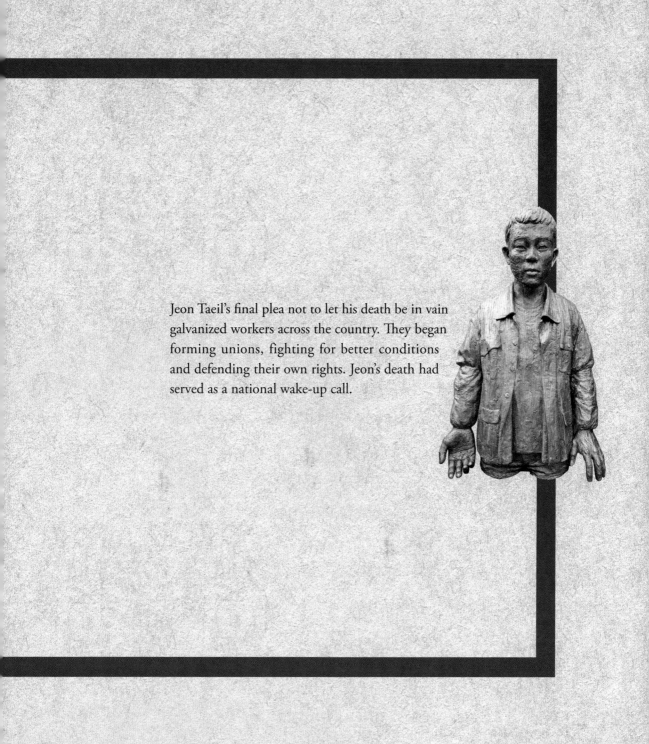

TIME LINE	1943	1945	1948
	Colonial period	**USAMGIK**	**USAMGIK**
	Government-General introduces forced mobilization and conscription	Liberation (August 15)	Kim Gu visits North Korea; makes declaration in Pyeongyang

"Reach for the 1980s! 10 billion won in exports, $1,000 in per capita income"

This slogan, printed on a banner that hung at the entrance to my middle school, was the first thing I saw every morning. Today, Korea's per capita is more than US $30,000, but in those days it was barely one thirtieth of that. The government had launched a campaign aimed at spurring on the whole country to reach the magic $1,000 mark. Somebody even came up with a special song:

"Oh, the good life, the good life! Soon, we'll be living it too!"

After the Korean War armistice in 1953, South Korea began working furiously to heal the deep scars left by the conflict. Most urgent of all was the task of economic recovery. Koreans longed to overcome the hunger and poverty that reigned at this time by building a more prosperous society.

Let's see how they achieved economic development, and how hard they worked for their success.

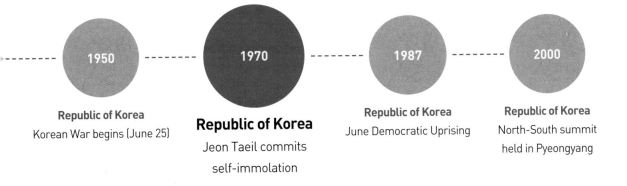

1950

Republic of Korea

Korean War begins (June 25)

1970

Republic of Korea

Jeon Taeil commits
self-immolation

1987

Republic of Korea

June Democratic Uprising

2000

Republic of Korea

North-South summit
held in Pyeongyang

In the aftermath of the war, the United States helped Korea to revive its economy, providing rice, wheat and barley for free and funding the construction of new factories. This aid came in the form of grants; no repayment was demanded.

In fact, the help did not come without strings attached. The US had aims of its own: in exchange for the aid, South Korea was to become an unquestioning ally of America. The country received some US $2.1 billion worth of aid in the eight years immediately after the war.

Rapid economic growth really took off in the 1960s. This was when foreigners starting coming out with phrases like

Delivering aid
The US provided commodities such as rice, barley, wheat, wheat flour and maize as aid after the Korean War. Huge quantities of flour poured into the country, in particular.

the "Miracle on the Hangang" and the "Dragon of Asia" to describe Korea's break-neck development. This remarkable transformation took place under the leadership of former military men, headed by president Park Chunghee.

ⓘ 'Jajangmyeon' - noodles born of US food aid

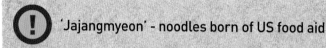

Jajangmyeon, cheap but filling noodles in black bean sauce, is Korea's most popular "Chinese" dish. Strangely, though, nothing resembling it can be found in China. *Jajangmyeon* was born in Korea, through a particular set of circumstances. Chinese food first came to Joseon in 1882. Qing forces sent to Seoul in response to the Imo Incident were followed by Chinese merchants, who introduced their country's cuisine. After liberation, the Korean government banned Chinese merchants in the country from trading. In the search for new work, several former traders opened restaurants. Gradually, they adapted certain Chinese dishes to suit Korean tastes.

Flour bag
The message on this bag reads "This flour is a gift from the people of America. Do not sell or barter it."
– National Folk Museum of Korea

Using common Korean ingredients like carrots and onions, the cheap wheat flour that had suddenly become available in such abundance, and thinned out *chunjang* (fermented black bean sauce), they created *jajangmyeon*. It was thanks to American aid that Koreans had access to so much flour at the time. The US provided more wheat than any other commodity, driving Korean flour prices down. *Jajangmyeon* would almost certainly not have become so popular if wheat flour had been more expensive. It can therefore be seen as a product of US aid after liberation.

A major general in the ROK Army, Park became president after leading a military coup in 1961. He began running the country in quasi-military fashion. Economic development was achieved on the same basis: setting a goal, then stopping at nothing until it was reached.

Spectacular growth

Park Chunghee's government led the country through four five-year plans, achieving development at a remarkable pace. This rapid growth drove up national income and exports by leaps and bounds. The former rose from US $33 million in 1960 to $10 billion in 1970. Factories worked at full capacity, while an expressway was built between Seoul and Busan, reducing the journey time from several days to just a few hours. Named the Gyeongbu [Seoul-Busan] Expressway, the road became a symbol of Korea's rapid growth. The country's first steelworks, shipyards and car factories opened. Many Koreans went to work overseas, with construction engineers working on projects in the Middle East and miners and

The Pony
First produced in 1975, this Korean-made car was a hit. I've been in several myself.
–Collection of Lee Ilhyeok

Gyeongbu Expressway
opening ceremony
Park Chunghee and first
lady Yuk Youngsoo cut the
tape at this ceremony on
July 7, 1970.

nurses emigrating to Germany.

Apartments, a novel type of housing, appeared in Seoul, while Cheonggyecheon Stream, which flowed through the center of the city, was covered with concrete and a raised expressway.

In rural villages, the government's New Community Movement brought unprecedented development. I still remember its theme song, which used to play in the streets and alleyways when I was young: "The dawn bell rings, a new day begins. Let's rise, shine and rebuild our villages. If we work hard, our communities will prosper!" They say Park Chunghee wrote the song himself.

New Community Village Movement slogans
and 'Saemaeul' ('New Community') magazine
This movement aimed to raise rural living standards. It brought huge
change to many rural villages, but was not without its problems.
– National Folk Museum of Korea

The New Community Movement transformed the country's villages beyond recognition. Thatched roofs were replaced by colorful tiles, streets grew wider, rivers and streams were lined with concrete banks. But it wasn't without its own problems. Poverty in farming villages is due to low incomes, but the New Community Movement focused more on improving outer appearances than on actually raising income. A new cultivar of rice called Tongil ("unification") was developed, greatly improving crop yields. Everyone lived frugally and worked hard. The old "slow and steady" mantra was swept away by "*ppalli ppalli*!" the ubiquitous exhortation to get things done as fast as possible.

Jeon Taeil: a beautiful young man

The process of achieving so much development in such a short time produced victims. Those who bore the greatest burden were the country's workers, especially teenage girls and young women. Girls not even fifteen years old would work twelve-hour a day, or take night shifts for a pitifully small salary. Many of them developed lung disease or other illnesses that slowly killed them due to atrocious working conditions. They simply worked themselves to the bone, barely even aware of what day it was. Have you ever heard *Sagye* ("Four Seasons")? Now a popular song, it was originally written to describe the feelings of young girls working the sewing machines all day long at garment factories:

Even when the red and yellow flowers bloom in the fields,
Even when the white butterflies sit on the sunlit wall,
Even when the warm spring wind blows across the mountainside,
My sewing machine keeps on turning.

With the country under quasi-military control, the workers had no way of appealing or protesting. They simply had to keep their heads down and endure their plight. One day, however, a garment cutter at Pyeonghwa Market named Jeon Taeil decided the world had to know about the plight of Korea's miracle workers.

Conditions in a sewing factory
Economic growth brought several problems, principally unequal distribution of the country's hard-won new wealth. Workers made the biggest sacrifices, especially teenage girls and young women.

Pyeonghwa Market was part of a sprawling complex of wholesale clothes shops and factories by Cheonggyecheon Stream. Labor was provided largely by teenage girls who had come to Seoul from the countryside to make a living. They slept and ate in the attic spaces above the workshops, working day and night and with no days off. Their workplaces were dark and dusty, and the girls were underfed, sleep-deprived and overworked. Many of them were slowly dying in these terrible conditions.

As a garment cutter, Jeon had a slightly higher income, but the young girls in the factories were being thoroughly exploited while receiving only a few thousand won each month. If they grew ill, they were fired.

One day, Jeon happened to come across the Labor Standard Law, a piece of legislation that set standards for working conditions in order to guarantee a basic level of welfare for workers. Pleased at his discovery, he bought a copy of the law and studied it closely. It clearly stated that workers should work no more than eight hours each day, and should be given days off on Sundays and public holidays.

How good it would be, Jeon thought, if the factory workers were granted the conditions described in this basic law. No more, no less: just the minimum legal standards. He called together the garment cutters in the market and created what he called the Fools' Association.

The Labor Standard Law
This law establishes certain standards for working conditions, with the aim of guaranteeing a basic standard of living for workers and introducing an element of balance to national development. First enacted in 1953, it has since undergone several amendments. The law sets standards regarding working hours, pay, public holidays and personal vacation time, termination of employment, compensation for industrial injury, and the formation of labor unions.

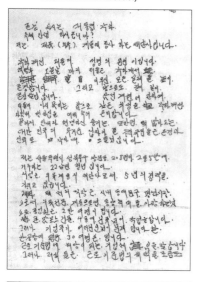

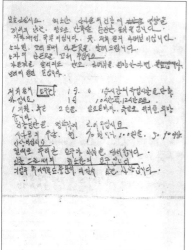

"We are human beings. But until now, we haven't been living like them. We've allowed ourselves to be treated like machines, and that makes us fools," he explained. "But if we wake up to our predicament and take control of our lives, we can make things better…"

Jeon then conducted a survey of working conditions at Pyeonghwa Market. 126 of the respondents worked between fourteen and sixteen hours a day; ninety-six were suffering from tuberculosis or another respiratory illness; and 102 had stomach disorders. Many also had eye problems due to working in dim lamplight. The garment cutter wrote a petition based on his survey findings and submitted it to the Ministry of Labor, along with several suggestions.

Jeon's proposals included reduced working hours, health checks for workers, increased wages, demolition of the attic spaces, installation of ventilators, replacement of lighting systems, guaranteed menstrual leave, and the formation of a labor union. Despite the basic nature of these suggestions, Jeon received no response from either his company or the Ministry of Labor.

"We won't achieve anything this way," Jeon told his colleagues at the Fools' Association. "Let's burn copies of the Labor Standard Law, since it's completely useless anyway."

The disgruntled workers agreed to Jeon's proposal. Privately, though he had other thoughts: just burning copies of the law was not enough. Nobody would take any notice unless a real sacrifice was made. Somebody had to die if the workers were to be taken seriously and have a chance of living better lives.

We are not machines!

On the morning of November 12, 1970, Jeon ironed his black work uniform and put on his best shoes. He lived near an old public cemetery at the foot of Dobongsan, a mountain that wraps around the upper fringes of Seoul. This was a poor neighborhood of densely built, unauthorized slums.

"You look smart today," his mother said. "Going somewhere special?"

"Mom, I really need to do something big to bring about change at the market."

"What? Why does it have to be you? Can't you just keep your head down a bit longer? Until you're thirty, at least? Think of your poor mom."

"Come and watch what happens in front of the bank by the market at one o'clock tomorrow afternoon. You might not see me for a long time after that."

"What d'you mean?"

Film 'Areumdaun cheongnyeon Jeon Taeil' The title of this biopic translates as "Jeon Taeil: A Beautiful Young Man." Jeon is also sometimes known as "The Workers' Friend" for making the ultimate sacrifice on their behalf.

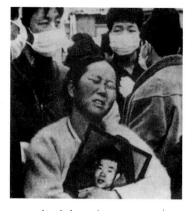

Jeon's funeral
Jeon's mother, Yi Soseon, weeps as she embraces a photo of her late son.

"After that, please carry on the campaign for better working conditions at Pyeonghwa Market instead of me."

Jeon didn't come home that night. At one o'clock the next day, some 500 workers from Pyeonghwa Market gathered outside the bank. They carried placards with the message, "We are not machines!"

Just when baton-wielding policemen had appeared and were starting to break up the protest, Jeon ran out from a nearby alleyway. His body was on fire.

"Observe the Labor Standard Law!" he shouted. "We are not machines! Let us rest on Sundays! Stop exploiting workers!"

He collapsed. Somebody threw a copy of the Labor Standard Law, which started burning alongside his body. He got up again.

"Don't let my death come to nothing!"

The rest of what Jeon said was incomprehensible. An ambulance arrived and his charred body was taken away.

A few days later, Jeon died. He was twenty-three years old. His mother never forgot his plea that she carry on his campaign until it succeeded.

The labor movement begins

Jeon's final plea not to let his death be in vain galvanized workers across the country. They began forming unions, fighting for better conditions and defending their own rights. Jeon's death had served as a national wake-up call.

Today, most factories and companies of all sizes have labor unions to safeguard the rights of workers. The Labor Standard Law is followed much more closely than in Jeon's time. Workers are no longer pushed around or looked down upon like servants. All this is thanks to the movement started by the young garment cutter.

The story of Jeon's short life has been depicted in a book and a film, too. Indeed, what I've just told you comes from just that book: *Jeon Taeil pyeongjeon* ("A Critical Biography of Jeon Taeil"), by lawyer Jo Yeong-rae. When I was a student, just possessing this book was forbidden, but now even the film is openly screened. Things really have changed a lot. And this, too, is thanks to the sacrifice Jeon made.

Korean workers only became free to openly assert their rights less than twenty years ago. Since then, the number of migrant workers in the country has increased dramatically. Today, they endure some of the terrible hardships that Korean teenage girls once went through. We have a saying in Korean: "Frogs don't remember when they were tadpoles." A Korean looking down on migrant workers and treating them unfairly today is just as stupid as the frog who can't remember when she was a tadpole.

Bronze statue of Jeon Taeil In 2005, thirty-five years after Jeon's death, his statue was erected outside Pyeonghwa Market by Cheonggyecheon Stream in Seoul.

?!

Multicultural families, our new neighbors

Shafra is a young Bangladeshi girl. She came to Korea with her parents, who work in a factory. When she first started elementary school, Shafra couldn't speak a word of Korean. But now she speaks the language well and is highly independent. Her dream is to keep studying in Korea and become a teacher.

What makes Shafra sadder than anything is when her friends look down on her for coming from a poor country.

"It was my friend's birthday today, so her mom brought a cake for us to share," she says. "My friend asked me if we have cake in Bangladesh. And if we have cars. I told her: of course we do! My country has everything that Korea has. I like Korea, but my friends don't seem to like Bangladesh."

A group wedding for international couples
Here, nine couples get married in a joint ceremony to share the high cost of a wedding in Korea. The brides are from countries including China, Vietnam and Cambodia.

Migrant workers
There are currently around 500,000 migrant workers in Korea. They generally work in tough or dangerous jobs that Koreans prefer not to do.

Still, Shafra is relatively lucky. Some foreign children in Korea can't go to school at all, because their parents are unregistered workers, or so-called illegal aliens. These are foreigners who stay in the country after their visas have expired. Many of them come from countries poorer than Korea in order to earn money.

In 2003, the law was changed to allow the children of illegal aliens to go to elementary school. In reality, though, many of these children are unable to attend because of tough family circumstances or difficulties in adapting.

The number of foreigners in Korea is now around 1.5 million, while one or two out of every ten marriages produces an international couple. Living with foreigners is now a natural part of life in Korea, not some strange or unfamiliar experience. We often see non-Korean faces on the subway, and neighborhoods like Itaewon are full of restaurants selling food from all over the world. One neighborhood in Ansan, Gyeonggi-do, is home to many foreigners and has become known as the Village without Borders, while men in the countryside commonly marry women from Vietnam, Uzbekistan and other Asian countries. From now on, we'll be seeing many more children of mixed parentage.

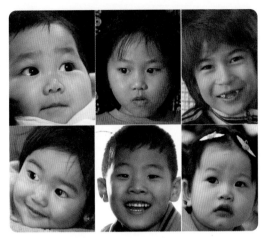

Children of multicultural families
Korea is set to see a growing number of children born to parents of different nationalities in the future. At the moment, almost 20,000 such children attend Korean elementary, middle and high school, the vast majority of them elementary school. There are more than 30,000 multicultural children of pre-school age.

Foreigners are now part of our communities, living alongside us. We live in what is called a multicultural society; households in which one parent is Korean and the other foreign are known as multicultural families. What's the point of looking down on people because their skin color is different or they come from a country poorer than Korea? How would you feel if that happened to you in a country richer than Korea? We can only pride ourselves on a truly international society when we accept foreigners for who they are and treat them with due respect.

CHAPTER 16

The struggle for democracy

"Call another election," they chanted.

"Down with Syngman Rhee!"

"Down with dictatorship!"

Once again, the police opened fire on the demonstrators, but the latter refused to yield. Defying death, they carried on protesting, determined to bring down Rhee's dictatorship and restore proper democracy.

Some 200 people were shot dead by police, with around 6,000 more injured. But the demonstrations carried on the next day, and the day after that.

TIME
LINE

1943

Colonial period
Government-General
introduces forced mobilization
and conscription

1945

USAMGIK
Liberation (August 15)

1948

USAMGIK
Kim Gu visits North Korea;
makes declaration in
Pyeongyang

Democracy. Rule by the people, for the people, in a country that belongs to the people. Korean democracy has only been around for seventy years or so, and is still having a few teething problems. And it didn't come easily: many people fought and made huge sacrifices to win it. Today, I'd like to tell you how the seeds of democracy were sown and grew into the system we live in now. It all started with the April Revolution in 1960 and came to a head with the June Democratic Uprising in 1987.

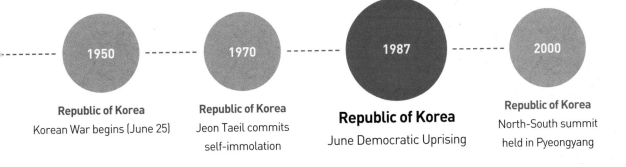

1950	1970	1987	2000
Republic of Korea	**Republic of Korea**	**Republic of Korea**	**Republic of Korea**
Korean War begins (June 25)	Jeon Taeil commits self-immolation	June Democratic Uprising	North-South summit held in Pyeongyang

The Republic of Korea's fourth presidential election took place on March 15, 1960. By this time, some of the scars left by the Korean War were starting to heal. Syngman Rhee and Lee Kipoong, both of the Liberal Party, were elected president and vice president, respectively. This was to be Rhee's fourth consecutive term. After taking office as the first president of the newly established republic, he had remained in power ever since 1948.

When a single individual dominates government for this long in a democracy, it generally leads to trouble. In most democratic systems, the number of terms a president can serve is constitutionally limited.

Protest after the corrupt March 15 election
The presidential and vice-presidential elections of spring 1960 were dirty in the extreme. Ballot boxes were tampered with, vote counts altered, proxy votes cast, observers from opposition parties excluded from polling stations: every page of the corruption textbook was consulted. Syngman Rhee and Lee Kipoong were elected as a result.

Rhee resigns after fraudulent elections

Syngman Rhee ran the Republic of Korea as a dictatorship, ignoring the will of the people and doing more or less whatever he wanted. Corruption was rampant, the public was deeply unsatisfied and the economy was in crisis. So how on earth did Rhee get voted in again? He rigged the election.

The March, 1960, election was a sham of the worst kind. Votes were bought, voters were put into to groups of three and made to ensure that their fellow group members voted for Rhee, and ballot boxes were pre-stuffed with votes for him. Rhee and the Liberal Party's desire to cling to power drove them to resort to this compendium of dirty tricks.

The rigged election caused simmering public anger to boil over. The first protest occurred in the city of Masan, Gyeongsangnam-do Province.

"Call another election!" the demonstrators chanted. "Save democracy!"

The police opened fire indiscriminately on protestors, then falsely reported that the demonstration had been orchestrated by the communist party. Seven people were killed, seventy-three injured and twenty-six arrested.

About one month later, the body of a young man was pulled out of the sea near Masan. A tear gas canister was embedded in one of his eye sockets. The corpse was identified as that of Kim Juyeol, a student at Masan Commercial High School who had been missing since the March demonstrations. He had been killed when the canister, fired by police, hit him in the eye. The discovery caused an uproar in Masan and enraged its students. The news soon spread to the rest of the country.

A few days later, on April 18, some 3,000 students from Korea University held a demonstration outside the National Assembly in Seoul, demanding that those responsible for the Masan incident be punished. On their way back to the university, they were attacked by gangsters who had been put up to the task by Syngman Rhee and politicians in the Liberal Party.

Call another election!

The next day, April 19, was a Tuesday. Around 100,000 university, middle and high school students and other Seoulites took to the streets in protest.

"Call another election," they chanted.

"Down with Syngman Rhee!"

"Down with dictatorship!"

Kim Juyeol's corpse with tear gas canister
Kim died when a tear gas canister fired by police entered his eye socket. This wretched incident sparked the April Revolution.

Elementary school students join the protests
Even elementary school students took to the streets, brandishing a banner that read "Stop shooting our parents, brother and sisters!"

The April Revolution
Protesting crowds refused to back down even when fired on by the police. They continued to reject the election result, eventually bringing down the dictatorship of Syngman Rhee.

Once again, the police opened fire on the demonstrators, but the latter refused to yield. Defying death, they carried on protesting, determined to bring down Rhee's dictatorship and restore proper democracy.

Some 200 people were shot dead by police, with around 6,000 more injured. But the demonstrations carried on the next day, and the day after that. Soon, they had been going for a week. A group of some 400 sympathetic university professors from around the country joined the protestors, marching through the streets with Taegukgi banners held aloft.

"Take responsibility for the deaths of our students!" they chanted.

This show of support from professors, who commanded

Monument to the April Revolution
Students killed during the April
Revolution are buried here,
their graves lined up behind the
towering monument. Several of
the graves belong to students as
young as elementary school age.
The site bears silent witness to the
scale of the sacrifices made at this
time.

considerable respect in society, further encouraged the other demonstrators. The next day, they were back in the streets. Seoul buzzed with their energy for the rest of the month. Finally, on April 26, the embattled leader announced his resignation.

"I, Syngman Rhee, am resigning from the presidency and intend to spend the rest of my life as an ordinary citizen dedicated to my country and my people."

Twelve years of dictatorship were over at last. This episode, when pent-up longing for genuine democracy finally burst into the open, is now known as the April Revolution. It was the first time in Asian history that a dictatorship had been brought by popular action.

A middle school girl's last letter

"Mother, I can't wait any longer so I'll have to leave without seeing you. Please don't blame me for taking part in the demo. If we don't do something, no one will. I know I'm still young. But I know what's right for our country and our people. ... You might be sad to see me demonstrating like this, but please try and be happy as I'm doing it for the future of our nation and the independence of our people. ..."

Jin Yeongsuk was a second-grade student at Hansung Girls' Middle School. When she had finished this letter, she went off to take part in the April demonstrations, where she lost her life. Many other elementary, middle and high-school students took part in the revolution that spring, including lots of girls.

While the April Revolution appeared at first glance to be a struggle against Syngman Rhee's dictatorship, it was also infused with desire for democracy, national autonomy free from foreign interference, and reunification. But while the revolution succeeded in removing Rhee from power, a lot more time and effort were needed before the people of Korea finally secured true democracy and autonomy.

The May 16 coup d'état
At dawn on May 16, 1961, the year after the April Revolution, troops under the command of Major General Park Chunghee occupied the Capitol building and the headquarters of the Korean Broadcasting Company. Here, Park stands in the middle wearing dark glasses. He soon became president.

The dark years of Yusin

The dictatorship brought down by the April Revolution was soon replaced by another. The man in charge this time was Park Chunghee, who took power in a military coup on May 16, 1961. The new leader played an important role in developing the Korean economy while stifling democracy.

The Yusin Constitution is proclaimed
The new constitution was promulgated at this ceremony in the Capitol building on December 27, 1972.

Park spent seventeen years in power: even longer than Syngman Rhee. This may seem absurd to you, but when I was young I thought Park Chunghee was not just a president but the president - it was unimaginable that anyone else could ever hold the position. He was president from the day I was born until after I graduated high school. I only realized there was something wrong with this when I got to university.

Park established himself as a dictator, amending the constitution to suit his own needs. The worst years of his dictatorship were those under the Yusin Constitution, which Park introduced himself. *Yusin* literally means "renewal." Under the new constitution, all criticism of the government was banned. Those who defied this restriction were arrested and sent to jail.

Even Park Chunghee's dictatorship eventually reached the end of the road, however. At around 7:35 in the evening of October 26, 1979, shots rang out from a safe house in Gungjeong-dong, the Seoul neighborhood in which Cheong Wa Dae, the presidential office, is located. Park was having

The Yusin Era
In October, 1972, Park Chunghee declared martial law and announced plans to introduce a new constitution. This event is sometimes called the "October Yusin." The key provisions of the new constitution were that the president would be chosen by an electoral college called the National Council for Unification, rather than through direct elections, and that his or her powers would be greatly increased. This was a big step backwards for democracy.

The military crackdown
The government sent not regular troops but elite paratroopers to break up the Gwangju protests. They acted with unspeakable cruelty, shooting and bayonetting even those who had nothing to do with the demonstrations.

dinner with his chief bodyguard, Cha Jicheol, chief presidential secretary Kim Gyewon and Korean Central Intelligence Agency chief Kim Jaegyu. As the men sat eating together, Kim Jaegyu had taken out a gun and shot Park and Cha. The dictator had been killed by one of his favorite men.

Militias fight against vicious suppression

With Park Chunghee dead, those who had opposed his dictatorship went into action to prepare for proper democracy. The general desire for a democratic society was now stronger than ever; the military-style systems and ways of thought that had dominated under the Yusin Constitution began to collapse and disappear. People allowed themselves to hope that democracy was about to flourish again after a long absence.

Once again, however, it was not that easy. The military soon took power back into its own hands, led this time by Chun Doohwan. The move sparked protests across the country and further stoked the desire for democracy.

One spring day in May, 1980, a crowd of 100,000 students

and other citizens gathered in the square in front of Seoul Station to demand democracy. Their passion made the "Seoul Spring" seem hotter than a midsummer heatwave.

On May 18, a pro-democracy protest began in Gwangju, Jeollanam-do Province. This time, government troops were deployed and brutally put down the demonstrators. An eight-month pregnant woman waiting in the street for her husband was shot through the head by an army bullet; even children playing by a stream with their friends were mowed down. No one knows how many people died this way. "Not even the Korean War was this bad," some older people commented angrily.

The enraged people of Gwangju now united in protest. From middle- and high-school students to the elderly, they set out to defend their city and democracy. Many of them formed voluntary militias to fight against the government troops. The battle continued for nine days, from May 18 to 27.

Witnessing Gwangju
Dong-a ilbo journalist Kim Yeongtaek gave the following testimony about what he saw in Gwangju: "When the commander gave the order to arrest everyone in the street, the paratroopers fixed bayonets onto their guns and charged at the citizens. They beat them indiscriminately; those that collapsed were dragged away like dogs and put onto a truck. ... I even saw a young couple get dragged away, stamped on by soldiers in boots and clubbed in the face until they were covered in blood."

No one outside Gwangju had any inkling of what was going on there, however. Newspapers and the television did report that something they called the "Gwangju incident" was in progress, but the way they described it was far from the truth. Most of them ran nonsensical stories about brave government troops entering a lawless city to put down riots led by "hooligans and commies."

It took nine whole years for an accurate picture to emerge of what had happened in Gwangju that spring. In 1989, the truth behind the incident was finally acknowledged at a National Assembly hearing. But those who ordered the army to crush the demonstrations—those responsible for ruining so many lives in Gwangju—have yet to take any responsibility for their actions.

The number of those killed and injured during the Gwangju Democratization Movement is still unknown. In addition to those harmed physically, many were so traumatized by the events that May that they required psychiatric help or became unable to lead normal lives.

Direct presidential elections

The flame of democracy once again attempted to burn in June 1987, when Roh Taewoo, another army general, emerged as a candidate to take over the presidency from Chun Doohwan.

At the time, the president was not chosen through popular elections but indirectly, by an electoral college. This may seem absurd to you now, but that's how things were. The system had been introduced by Park Chunghee as part of his Yusin Constitution. The electoral college did not choose one of several candidates; rather, a single figure was nominated and the college voted to approve or reject her or him. Under this system, Park Chunghee was approved for a fourth term in office by a record-breaking 2,357 out of 2,359 votes, with two spoilt ballots. If Roh Taewoo had been put into office by this system, the Korean people would have spent three decades ruled by military men who came to power through military force. They were now truly sick of dictatorship.

From around June 10, 1987, a mixture of citizens, students and workers took to the streets to call for the end of dictatorship. All manner of ordinary people joined in, from smartly-dressed office workers to women with shopping bags. Almost every day, Jongno, one of the main streets in downtown Seoul, echoed with cries for democracy. This

The June Democratic Uprising
This popular movement in 1987 succeeded in winning direct presidential elections after fourteen years. This system remains in place today. This photo shows the funeral of Lee Hanyeol, a Yonsei University student whose death from fragments of a tear gas canister provoked anger that further fueled the uprising.

episode is often known as the June Democratic Uprising.

Finally, on June 29, presidential candidate Roh Taewoo announced that he would amend the constitution to allow direct presidential elections. This became known as the June 29 Declaration; since then, all South Korean presidents have been directly elected.

The democracy in Korea today is the result of a gradual evolution through the April Revolution, the Gwangju Democratization Movement, and the June Democratic Uprising. Many people have been killed, injured and imprisoned along the way. The freedom and happiness they won for today's Korea must never be taken for granted.

That's as far as I'll go for today. There's plenty more left to say, but no need to say it all at once. Instead, let me share one of my favorite songs with you: a song that came to symbolize the campaign for democracy in Korea.

The path we're sworn to follow

is one without love, fame or glory.

Many comrades have fallen, leaving only flags in the wind.

Let us march on, unwavering, towards the new dawn.

The years may pass by, but the mountains and rivers bear witness.

Now we rise up again, our cries ever louder.

Follow us as we take the lead.

Follow us as we take the lead.

Democracy and the World Cup

2002 World Cup The World Cup provided another big surprise when hordes of young Koreans began wearing the now-famous red T-shirts. To older South Koreans, who had for decades associated this color with communism and North Korea, witnessing a sea of red-clad compatriots outside Seoul City Hall was a huge shock. In the end, the event helped rid South Korean society of its so-called "red complex."

Anyone in Korea in June, 2002 will remember the euphoric World Cup fever that gripped the country. Much of downtown Seoul filled with a sea of fans in red T-shirts, red scarfs and Taegeukgi patterns painted on their faces. Over and over, they cheered for their home country: "Dae-han Min-guk!!!"

Seldom had the name of the Republic of Korea echoed through its own streets like this. Everyone, from the youngsters by City Hall and in Gwanghwamun to the families at home and the people gathered around TV screens in restaurants across the nation, came together. What had sent them wild like this? Surely it was something more than football? I think it was. I believe the scenes of ecstasy we witnessed that summer were the release of something normally suppressed by Koreans in their everyday lives. A thirst for freedom, or for change. I think the World Cup provided them with a pretext to let these pent-up feelings out for once.

This longing for freedom and change had been building up for many years. During thirty years of dictatorship, military leaders had severely repressed the freedom and creativity of their people. This is why the administration of Kim Youngsam, the new president inaugurated in 1992, was welcomed by the people as the first civilian government in thirty years. Whatever the government calls itself or is labelled by others, the important thing is whom it really serves and what its aims are. Korean democracy is still in its infancy and taking its first, faltering steps. Soon, it must learn to run, powerfully, on its own two feet. And it's up to the next generation to ensure that that happens.

CHAPTER 17

Encounters
for reunification

The 2002 Asian Games in Busan provided an opportunity for rapprochement between the two Koreas. Fans from each side answered each others' cheers in the stadium.

"We...!" the South Koreans chanted. "...are one nation!" the North's fans shouted in response.

When the Northerners chanted "Reunification...!" the Southerners responded with "...for the motherland!"

For an exceptional moment, North and South Korea really did become one.

Both sides' flags waved side by side in the stadium.

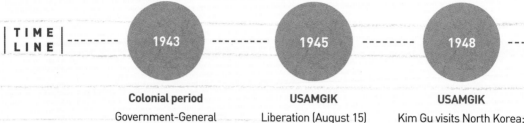

TIME LINE

1943 ···· 1945 ···· 1948 ·············

Colonial period
Government-General
introduces forced mobilization
and conscription

USAMGIK
Liberation (August 15)

USAMGIK
Kim Gu visits North Korea;
makes declaration in
Pyeongyang

One of the most remarkable things that ever happened to my family took place while we were queueing to enter Red Square in Moscow. When we spotted a group of North Koreans not far ahead of us, my young daughter plucked up the courage to walk over and say hello. She greeted the fat man at the head of the group, then offered him her hand to shake. After what seemed like a moment of hesitation, the man took her small hand in his huge one. My daughter ran back to us, her heart thumping with excitement. She was momentarily lost for words, but then she spoke:

"When I grow up, I'm going to reunify Korea. I'll become the sort of person we need for reunification."

This was the most memorable part of our whole trip to Russia: North Koreans feel so distant — slightly scary, even — when we're at home in the South, but bumping into them abroad gives us a happy sense of familiarity.

Today, let's take a look at North Korea and the lives of its people.

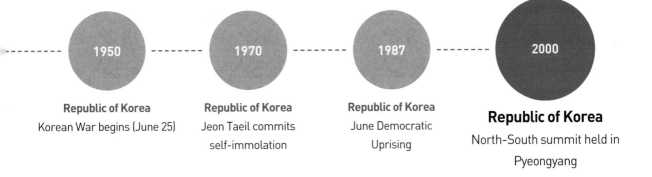

1950	1970	1987	2000
Republic of Korea	**Republic of Korea**	**Republic of Korea**	**Republic of Korea**
Korean War begins (June 25)	Jeon Taeil commits self-immolation	June Democratic Uprising	North-South summit held in Pyeongyang

You must be curious about North Korea. How do its people live? What do they talk about with their friends? How do they spend their free time? What do they eat? Do they listen to pop music, like us? What kind of relationships do North Koreans have with their families, friends and colleagues? Our list of questions could go on forever.

Seoul (left) and
Pyeongyang (right)
The respective capitals of
South and North Korea.

Life in North Korea differs in many ways from that in the South. Korea has been divided into two separate states for more than seventy years now, which is quite enough time for significant differences to arise. The South has taken a capitalist path; the North, one of socialism. South Koreans have experienced an influx of American culture and been deeply influenced by US systems, attitudes and customs. The Soviet Union had a similar effect on North Korean society.

Nonetheless, the two states still have plenty of things in common. We both sing folk songs like *Arirang*, and we both celebrate Seollal and Chuseok, the Lunar New Year and harvest festival. We both consider rice, soup and kimchi to be the basis of a proper meal; we both wear traditional *hanbok* clothing on special occasions. And we speak the same language, albeit with slight variations in accent and vocabulary. Grandparents in both Koreas love their grandchildren, and all Koreans love singing and dancing.

Children in North Korea

You may have seen North Korean children on television, wearing red scarves. These, along with blouses for girls and shirts for boys, are not school uniforms but those of the Korean Youth Corps. North Korean children automatically become members of the corps when they reach the second

Public holidays in North Korea
In addition to Seollal and Chuseok, North Koreans observe the traditional holidays of Hansik and Dano, on April 6 and May 5 according to the lunar calendar, respectively. But the most important national holiday for them is without a doubt Kim Ilsung's birthday, on April 15, also known as the "Day of the Sun." Liberation Day (August 15) is also celebrated as a public holiday. Reportedly, North Korea recently started marking National Foundation Day (October 3), too.

grade of "elementary school." There, they learn about things like camping and communal life: it's not unlike boy or girl scout groups in other countries.

South Korean youngsters start at kindergarten, then progress through six years of elementary school, three years of middle school, three years of high school and four years of university. In North Korea, they spend two years at kindergarten (one in "lower class," one in "upper class"), four years at elementary school, six years at "senior middle school" (four in the middle school grades and two in the senior school grades) and four years at university.

North Korean senior middle school differs from its South Korean equivalents in that students spend six years in the same class, with the same class teacher. In South Korea, classes change every year and students have to get used to a new teacher and new friends. The North's system has the advantage that you can form strong bonds with your teacher and classmates over time, but also the drawback that you might grow bored of them. And if you don't get on with anyone in the class, you might be in for a lonely six years...

But do North Korean schools have outcasts like that too? Yes, apparently. They're known as "corner kids,"

Korean Youth Corps members
These scarves symbolize membership of the Korean Youth Corps, which was founded in 1946. All North Korean children become members when they reach the second grade of elementary school; from the fourth year of senior middle school, they enter the Kim Il Sung Socialist Youth League instead.

North Korean students studying English
Children in North Korea also consider learning English to be very important.

implying that their exclusion drives them into the corner of the room. Anyone who shows off too much, is messy or has bad habits that annoy other students might end up becoming a corner kid.

Do North Korean kids play computer games like their counterparts south of the border? Computers are rare and expensive in the North, so not many families have one and kids don't have the option of staying at home playing video games all day. Still, the country has its own computer whizzes. Elementary school students who show a particular aptitude for computing are chosen to study at places like Mangyongdae Schoolchildren's Palace, Pyongyang Students' and Children's Palace, or the specialist computing class at Kumsong Middle School, where they immerse themselves in programming.

Cartoons and 'Top 10' pop charts

Do they watch cartoons in North Korea, then? Of course. In fact, while young South Koreans watch plenty of imported cartoons, North Korea mostly produces its own. They are of quite a high standard, too: you can sometimes catch a glimpse of them in the South, too, at places like Imjingak.

Cartoons are known as "children's films" in the North. Popular works there have included *Sonyeon jangsu* ("The

North Korean cinema
North Koreans are big film lovers. Their government, too, wholeheartedly encourages the production of films, regarding them as an ideal means of influencing public opinion. In fact, it even makes the viewing of some films compulsory for its people. These include works such as *Joseon-ui byeol* ("Star of Korea") and *Minjok-ui unmyeong* ("Destiny of the Nation"), both biopics of Kim Ilsung. The North Korean film *Pulgasari* was even screened in South Korean movie theaters.

Boy General"), which depicts the adventures of Soeme, a young military commander in Goguryeo; *Yeongnihan neoguri* ("The Clever Raccoon Dog"), starring a cute raccoon dog and his animal friends; and *Hodong Wangja-wa Nangnang Gongju* ("Prince Hodong and Princess Nangnang").

And North Koreans love celebrities, too. Many youngsters see them as idols. The most

North Korean cartoons
This is a scene from *Horangi-reul igin goseumdochi* ("The Hedgehog Who Beat the Tiger"), a cartoon produced by the North's Korean Science and Educational Film Studio (also known as SEK Studio). The popular children's film tells the story of a little hedgehog who manages to defeat a tiger, the mighty king of the jungle.

popular celebrities are given titles such as *inmin baeu* or *gonghun baeu*, meaning "people's actor/actress" and "distinguished actor/actress," respectively, in recognition of their talents on the silver screen or in revolutionary operas. Top celebrities include Jeon Hyeyeong, the singer who sang hit pop song *Hwiparam* ("Whistle") and Jo Cheongmi, female star of the revolutionary opera *Pibada* ("Sea of Blood"). Revolutionary operas are similar to Western operas. North Koreans consider them just as important as films.

What about pop charts? In 2001, North Korean newspaper *Minju joseon* ("Democratic Korea") published a list of "10 hit songs" of the previous decade. The list included tracks like *Hiwparam*, *Udeungbul* ("Bonfire"), *Nae ireum mutji maseyo*

'People's athlete' Kye Sunhi
Kye won the gold medal in the
Extra Lightweight women's judo at
the Atlanta Olympics in 1996.

("Don't Ask My Name"), *Tongil Arirang* ("Unification Arirang") and *Cheonyeo sijeol kkot sijeol* ("Youth Is Like a Flower").

Athletes who achieve victory for North Korea are designated "*inmin cheyugin*" ("people's athletes"); one example is Kye Sunhi, who won the gold medal in the Extra Lightweight women's judo event at the 1996 Summer Olympics in Atlanta.

Why should Korea be reunified?

A surprising number of the young Koreans I've met seem unsure whether reunification is really necessary. You yourself may have Korean friends who hold this view. Perhaps they find life in South Korea to be quite satisfactory and can't see any reason for their country to be joined with the North again. Some of them may even actively oppose reunification, on the grounds that it would land South Korea with the heavy burden of looking after everyone currently over the border in the North.

So what benefits would reunification bring? Firstly, a solution to the current problems associated with national division, not least of which are its high military and other costs.

If we no longer needed to spend so much on defense due to national division, the money could be used instead for economic development or social welfare, helping the unemployed, the elderly and orphans, or put into a national pension fund. And there would be no more need for the national system of compulsory military service that forces young men to spend two

A reunion for divided families
No one felt the impact of national division more than families split apart by the new North-South border. Many of them are only granted the briefest of reunions, decades after separation, when they are already nearing the end of their lives. How painful must it be for them to say goodbye again once these short meetings are over?

years in the armed forces when they could be studying or working instead.

You may recall that the two Koreas are technically still at war, and could resume hostilities at any time. Reunification would remove this risk, too. And it would allow divided families to come together again. Above all, it would create a unified Korea with far more potential as a player on the world stage, by combining the current technology and wealth of the South with the natural and human resources of the North. A reunified Korea could be much better off.

But would reunification really mean that South Korea had to finance the North? Perhaps this depends on how the country is put back together. The South would be forced to support the North if reunification meant dismantling the latter completely and recreating it according to the same systems and society as the former. That would involve rebuilding all the North's factories and other facilities, and teaching its people to think just like Southerners. Known as "reunification by absorption," this model would mean one Korea taking over the other entirely on its own terms.

But there are other ways, too. If a more balanced arrangement could be agreed upon, with each side respecting the differences between South and North and agreeing to recognize each other's good points, the South could avoid taking complete responsibility for financing a unilaterally

(!) 'Cultural language,' North Korea's standard dialect

Standard Korean in the South is officially defined as the modern speech of the Seoul area. The North's equivalent is the Pyeongyang regional dialect. But instead of labeling this "standard Korean," the North Korean government calls it *munhwaeo* ("cultural language"). While South Korea now uses countless loanwords from English and other languages, or newly-synthesized Sino-Korean terms, to refer to new objects and phenomena, the North has created more than 50,000 words based on pure Korean language to describe things as diverse as strollers, wigs, parking lots, frying pans and bras. These may sound quaint and sometimes comical to South Koreans, but it's true that they help protect the North Korean language from a flood of imported words.

There are also a few differences in the way South and North Koreans pronounce numbers, especially in the use of pure Korean numbers instead of their Sino-Korean equivalents when counting some units of measurement.

Preparations for a joint North-South Korean 'dictionary of unification' The language spoken in South and North Korea differs more and more with the passing of time. In order to overcome this phenomenon, linguists from both sides of the DMZ decided to get together and produce a *Gyeoremal-keunsajeon* ("Unabridged and Unified Korean Dictionary") They aim to complete it by 2019.

North Korea viewed from Goseong Unification Observatory
Nearby North Korea can easily be seen with the naked eye
from this observatory in Goseong, Gangwon-do Province. If only
reunification itself were as close as this land, just across the DMZ.

absorbed North.

And it might surprise you to know that North Korea wasn't always as poor as it is now. It enjoyed higher living standards than the South in the 1960s, having kickstarted its economy faster after the Korean War. It was able to do this thanks to its abundant natural resources and skilled workers.

From the 1970s, however, South Korea's economic development gathered pace and the North began falling behind. You may associate it today with images of starving children, but that wasn't always the case, either. It only began lacking food after a series of serious droughts and floods in the early 1990s. Meanwhile, trade embargoes imposed by the US placed further strain on the North'

Kaesong Industrial Complex
North Korea has created special economic zones in several regions and is attempting economic development based on acceptance of capitalism. Gaesong Industrial Complex is one example of this. This photo shows the complex under construction.

s economy.

Today, North Korea is gradually recognizing some of the advantages of capitalism and working to develop its economy. It allows factories and companies run on capitalist terms to operate in special economic zones in places such as Rason, Nampo and Sinuiju, and at Kaesong Industrial Complex.

Until North and South become one...

The 2002 Asian Games in Busan provided an opportunity for rapprochement between the two Koreas. Fans from each side answered each others' cheers in the stadium.

"We…!" the South Koreans chanted. "…are one nation!" the North's fans shouted in response.

When the Northerners chanted "Reunification…!" the Southerners responded with "…for the motherland!"

For an exceptional moment, North and South Korea really did become one. Both sides' flags waved side by side in the stadium. The sight of North Korean flags flying in the Southern sky was amazing—when I was young, it would have been absolutely unthinkable. They seemed like a visual symbol of rapprochement between the two Koreas.

Many of us who have traveled abroad and introduced ourselves as Koreans get asked the question, "North or

South Korea?" To foreigners, these are two clearly separate countries.

Once, though, South Korea and North Korea really did come together to become simply "Korea." This happened at the 1991 World Table Tennis Championships in Japan, which the two Koreas entered as a single team. This team even ended up defeating China, the tournament favorites, in the women's team event. The victory offered all Koreans a glimpse of the potential of their country after reunification—if only North and South Korea could combine forces beyond

Fans at the Asian Games in Busan
Here, North and South Korean fans cheer together, waving Korean Unification flags and singing Arirang.

North and South Korean athletes carry the Korean Unification Flag At the opening ceremony of the Sydney Summer Olympics in 2000, the national teams of both Koreas entered the stadium together, carrying the Korean Unification Flag. Imagine what could be achieved if the two states joined forces in other areas, too.

the world of table tennis.

After our chance encounter with North Koreans in Moscow, my daughter wrote about it in her diary:

"When I shook hands with the man with the big Kim Ilsung badge on his chest, I realized: 'So North Koreans have warm hands, too!' When I let go, I felt a pang of regret. Korea really should be unified. I think combining North Korea's resources and our technology would bring us faster economic development. The North Koreans probably don't like being the objects of our pity. Surely it would be better if both Koreas cooperated while recognizing each other's strengths. Europeans cross borders freely into each other's countries—I wish we could coexist with North Korea like

Nature in the Demilitarized Zone
This zone, often known by its abbreviation, DMZ, was created as part of the armistice agreement that put Korean War hostilities on hold. It extends two kilometers to each side of the Military Demarcation Line. Only a few soldiers have had access to the DMZ over the past sixty years or so, leaving nature to thrive there. It is now a place of interest to ecologists worldwide.

that, recognizing each other's good points and cooperating together."

I have to say, I agree with my daughter. I hope the future will bring reconciliation between the two Koreas.

Toward reunification

"Head north for reunification!"

"Defeat the communists and reunify Korea!"

I grew up hearing slogans like these, calling for South Korea to reunite the nation by invading the North and overthrowing the Workers' Party of Korea. These days, things have changed. Hardly anyone advocates starting a war to bring the country back together: the

The June 15 North–South Joint Declaration
In June, 2000, North and South Korea's leaders held a historic meeting that produced the June 15 North–South Joint Declaration.

general desire is for peaceful reunification. People have realized that there is nothing to be gained from another war. North and South Korea have made various efforts for peaceful reunification over the years. The first came in 1972, more than forty years ago, when both sides issued the "July 4 North–South Joint Statement." This contained a commitment to autonomous and peaceful reunification, achieved by the two Koreas without foreign interference, and for unity as a nation despite the two sides' different political ideologies.

Later, in June 2000, then-South Korean president Kim Daejung and North Korean National Defence Commission chairman Kim Jongil held a summit meeting in Pyeongyang. This was the first encounter between the leaders of both Koreas since the division of their nation fifty-five years earlier. Here, they issued the "June 15 North–South Joint Declaration."

The new joint declaration also called for autonomous reunification based upon acknowledgment of and respect for each side's ideology and system. It made commitments to allow meetings between divided families and for contact and cooperation in a variety of fields including economics, culture, the arts, sport, society and the environment.

But while it's relatively easy for the two sides to make grand statements and declarations, the important thing is whether or not they actually keep the promises made. Even the most sweeping statement is meaningless unless it leads to action.

Six-party talks
If reunification is to be achieved, the influence of nearby global powers will be needed in addition to the efforts of North and South Korea. This photo shows representatives of South Korea, North Korea, the United States, China, Japan and Russia who have gathered for a round of "six-party talks." All of these states have stakes in the question of Korean reunification. In this respect, reunification is an international issue.

Index

Museum

National Folk Museum of Korea — May 10 Election poster 214 | Flour bag 246 | New Community Village Novement slogans and Saemaeul magazine 248

Samseong Museum of Publishing — Choe Namseon and handwritten manuscripts 188

Press

JungAng Ilbo — Ethnic Koreans in Sakhalin 126 | Coming Home 127 | The Berlin Wall 207 | Candlelight vigil for Hyosun and Miseon 240 | A group wedding for international couples 256 | Migrant workers 256 | Children of multicultural families 257

Newsis — People's athlete Kye Sunhi 282

Tongil news — North Korean students studying English 279

Yonhapnews — 2002 World Cup 273 | North and South Korean athletes carry the Korean Unification Flag 288 | The June 15 North-South Joint Declaration 290

Group and Private

Academy of Korean Studies, Encyclopedia of Korean Local Culture — Memorial stone for Sin Hyosun and Sim Miseon 241

Chun Taeil Memorial Society — Jeon Taeil's petition 252 | Jeon's funeral 254

Headquarters of Cheondoism — Eorini magazine 109

e-history — The Yusin Constitution is proclaimed 267

film company Giheoksidae — Areumdaun cheongnyeon Jeon Taeil 253

House of Sharing — Kkeullyeogam 186

Independence Hall of Korea — Text of the Protectorate Treaty 16 | Righteous Army of the Thirteen Provinces 33 | Righteous soldiers 34 | Sin Dolseok's army in action 37 | Patriotic books 40 | Newspapers and magazines that spearheaded the

Historical records and books

임병찬(林炳瓚), 대마도일기(對馬島日記), 《독립운동사자료집 2-의병항쟁사자료집》, 독립운동사편찬위원회, 1970

박한설 편, 애국선열 윤희순여사 기념사업추진위원회, 《외당선생삼세록(畏堂先生三世錄)》, 강원일보사, 1995

안중근(安重根), 《안중근의사 자서전》, 안중근의사숭모회, 1979

황현(黃玹), 허경진 옮김, 《매천야록(梅泉野錄)》, 한양출판, 1995

이정식.한홍구 엮음, 《항전별곡-조선독립동맹 자료 1》, 거름, 1986

단재신채호선생기념사업회 단재신채호전집간행위원회 편, 《단재(丹齋) 신채호(申采浩) 전집》 1-3, 형설출판사, 1982

박은식(朴殷植), 김도형 역주, 《한국통사(韓國痛史)》, 계명대학교출판부, 1997

박은식(朴殷植), 남만성 옮김, 《한국독립운동지혈사(韓國獨立運動之血史)》 상.하, 서문당, 1975

김준엽(金俊燁), 《장정(長征) 2 - 나의 광복군 시절 하(下)》, 나남출판, 2003

한국정신대문제대책협의회.한국정신대연구회 편, 《강제로 끌려간 조선인 군위안부들-증언집》 1-2, 한울, 1993-1997

이광수(李光洙), 《이광수 전집》 13,17, 삼중당, 1963

박수복, 엄마 따라 갈 거야 김숙희의 경우, 《핵의 아이들 - 86 한국 원폭피해자 2세의 현장》, 한국 기독교 가정생활사, 1986

김구(金九), 도진순 주해, 《백범일지(白凡逸志)》, 돌베개, 1997

우남이승만문서편찬위원회, 《이화장(梨花莊) 소장 우남(雩南) 이승만(李承晚) 문서(동문편(東文篇))》 1-3 이승만 저작, 중앙일보사.연세대학교 현대한국학연구소, 1998

구술 조윤하, 정리 이흥환, 1.20 판문점 포로들 - 내레 앞에총이 뭐인디두 몰랐다니까니, 《구술 한국 현대사》, 1986, 미완

한국현대사사료연구소 편, 《광주5월민중항쟁사료전집》, 풀빛, 1990

독립기념관 한국독립운동정보시스템 http://search.i815.or.kr/main.do

정일성, 《이토 히로부미-알려지지 않은 이야기들》, 지식산업사, 2002

윤덕한, 《이완용 평전》, 중심, 1999

이선준, 《일성 이준 열사》, 을지서적, 1994

김희곤, 《신돌석; 백년 만의 귀향》, 푸른역사, 2001

박성수, 《나철》, 북캠프, 2003

최은희, 《여성 전진 70년-초대 여기자의 회고》, 추계 최은희 전집 5, 조선일보사, 1991

김세일, 《홍범도》 1-5, 제3문학사, 1989-1990

윤병석, 《백야 김좌진》, 태극출판사, 1977

Матвей Тимофеевич Ким, *КОРЕЙСКИЕ ИНТЕРНАЦИОНАЛИСТЫ В БОРЬБЕ ЗА ВЛАСТЬ СОВЕТОВ НА ДАЛЬНЕМ ВОСТОКЕ(1918-1922)*, НАУКА,(1918-1922), НАУКА, 1979, 이준형 옮김, 《일제하 극동시베리아의 한인 사회주의자들》, 역사비평사, 1990

민윤식, 《소파 방정환 평전: 청년아, 너희가 시대를 아느냐》, 중앙M&B, 2003

손인수, 《한국교육사상가 평전》 2, 문음사, 1992

강덕상, 홍진희 옮김, 《조선인의 죽음: 관동대지진과 조선인 학살의 진상》, 동쪽나라, 1995

Владимир Ким, *ПРАВДА—ПОЛВЕКА СПУСТЯ*, УЗБЕКИСТОН, 1999, 김현택 옮김, 《러시아 한인 강제 이주사》, 경당, 2000

강만길, 《회상의 열차를 타고》, 한길사, 1999

안병직 편, 《신채호》, 한길사, 1979

최홍규, 《신채호의 민족주의 사상》, 단재 신채호선생 기념사업회, 1983

신용하, 《신채호의 사회사상연구》, 한길사, 1984

염인호, 《김원봉 연구》, 창작과비평사, 1992

홍인근, 《이봉창 평전》, 나남출판, 2002

이상재.윤규상, 《윤봉길》, 도솔, 1996

임종빈, 《천추의열 윤봉길》, 인물연구소, 1975

정수웅 엮음, 《최승희-격동의 시대를 살다간 어느 무용가의 생애와 예술》, 눈빛, 2004

강이향 엮음, 김채현 해제, 《최승희, 생명의 춤 사랑의 춤》, 지양사, 1993

박규원, 《상하이 올드데이스; 독립운동가의 아들로 태어나 중국의 영화 황제가 된 김염의 불꽃 같은 삶》, 민음사, 2003

스즈키 쓰네카쓰(鈴木常勝), 이상 옮김, 《상해의 조선인 영화황제》, 실천문학사, 1996

박경식, 박경옥 옮김, 《조선인 강제연행의 기록》, 고즈윈, 2008

Ruth Thomson, Terezin: *Voices from the Holocaust*, Candlewick Press, 2011

정운현 편역, 《창씨개명》, 학민사, 1994

송우혜, 《윤동주 평전》, 열음사, 1994

정용욱, 《존 하지와 미군 점령통치 3년》, 중심, 2003

이강수, 《반민특위 연구》, 나남출판, 2003

한국역사연구회 1930년대 연구반, 《일제하 사회주의운동사》, 한길사, 1991

이정박헌영기념사업회 편집, 임경석 글, 《이정 박헌영 일대기》, 역사비평사, 2004

김준엽.김창순, 《한국공산주의운동사》 1-5, 청계연구소, 1986

정병준, 《우남 이승만 연구》, 역사비평사, 2005

이기형, 《몽양 여운형》, 실천문학사, 1984

서중석, 《한국현대민족운동연구: 해방후 민족국가 건설운동과 통일전선》, 역사비평사, 1992

역사문제연구소.역사학연구소.제주4.3연구소.한국역사연구회 편, 제주 4.3 제50주년 기념사업추진 범국민위원회 간, 《제주 4.3 연구》, 역사비평사, 1999

노민영 편, 《잠들지 않는 남도-제주도 4.3항쟁의 기록》, 온누리, 1988

Bruce Cumings, *Origins of the Korean War: Liberation and the Emergence of Separate Regimes, 1945-1947*, Princeton University Press, 1981, 김자동 옮김, 《한국전쟁의 기원》, 일월서각, 1986

김학준, 《한국전쟁》, 박영사, 1997

한국정치연구회정치사분과 엮음, 《한국전쟁의 이해》, 역사비평사, 1990

박태균, 《한국전쟁》, 책과함께, 2005

권정생, 《몽실 언니》, 창작과비평사, 1984

전태일기념관건립위원회 엮음, 《어느 청년노동자의 삶과 죽음-전태일 평전》, 돌베개, 1983 /조영래, 《전태일 평전》, 돌베개, 2001

박채란, 《국경 없는 마을》, 서해문집, 2004

학민사 편집실 편, 《4.19의 민중사; 사월혁명자료집》, 학민사, 1984

광주매일 《정사(正史) 5.18》 특별취재반, 《정사 5.18》, 사회평론, 1995

이기춘 외, 《통일에 앞서 보는 북한의 가정생활문화》, 서울대학교출판부, 2001

황인태, 《통일정책론》, 조명문화사, 1995

이찬행, 《통일나라 북한 여행》, 아이세움, 2002

이찬행, 《통일나라 역사 여행》, 아이세움, 2003

이찬행, 《통일나라 문화유산 여행》, 아이세움, 2003

임수경, 《참 좋다! 통일세상》, 황소걸음, 2003

국사편찬위원회, 《한국사》 47-52, 2001-2002

한국정신문화연구원 편, 《해방전후사 사료 연구》 1.2, 선인, 2002

한국역사연구회 현대사연구반, 《한국현대사》 1-4, 풀빛, 1991

강만길, 《고쳐 쓴 한국현대사》, 창작과비평사, 1994

송건호 외, 《해방전후사의 인식》 1-4, 한길사, 1979-1989

박지향 외, 《해방전후사의 재인식》 1.2, 책세상, 2006

젊은역사연구모임, 《영화처럼 읽는 한국사》, 명진출판, 1999

박한용.장원정.황경, 《시와 이야기가 있는 우리 역사》 2, 동녘, 1996

전국역사교사모임, 《살아있는 한국사 교과서》, 휴머니스트, 2002

이기백, 《신수판(新修版) 한국사신론》, 일조각, 1994

변태섭, 《한국사 통론(通論)》, 삼영사, 1986

한국역사연구회, 《한국역사》, 역사비평사, 1992

한국사특강편찬위원회 편, 《한국사 특강》, 서울대학교 출판부, 1990

한국역사연구회, 《한국사강의》, 한울아카데미, 1989

역사문제연구소, 《사진과 그림으로 보는 한국의 역사》 3, 웅진출판, 1993

구로역사연구소, 《바로 보는 우리역사》 2, 거름, 1990

한국민중사연구회 편, 《한국민중사》 2, 풀빛, 1986

박석분.박은봉, 《인물여성사 한국편》, 새날, 1994

박은봉, 《한국사 상식 바로잡기》, 책과함께, 2007

박은봉, 《한권으로 보는 한국사 100장면》, 가람기획, 1993/ 《한국사 100장면》(개정판), 실천문학, 1997

박은봉, 《한국사 뒷이야기》, 실천문학사, 1997

박은봉, 《세계사 뒷이야기》, 실천문학사, 1994

박은봉, 《엄마의 역사편지》 2, 웅진주니어, 2000

Academic papers and essays

박한용.장원정.황경, 조선의 마지막 날, 《시와 이야기가 있는 우리 역사》 2, 동녘, 1996

박석두, 일제하 자영지주의 농가경제에 관한 연구-구례군 토지면 〈류씨가(柳氏家) 문서〉를 중심으로, 고려대 박사논문, 1998

배영순, 한말.일제초기의 토지조사와 지세개정에 관한 연구, 서울대 박사논문, 1988

이영훈, 토지조사사업의 수탈성 재검토, 《역사비평》 1993년 가을호

이현희, 의병장 면암 최익현 연구, 성신여자대학교 《연구논문집》 37, 2001

이정은, 3.1운동, 《한국사》 47, 국사편찬위원회, 2001

박민영, 봉오동 승첩과 청산리 대첩, 《한국사》 48, 국사편찬위원회, 2001

신용하, 홍범도 의병부대의 항일무장투쟁, 《한국민족운동사연구》 1, 1986

박환, 김좌진 장군의 항일독립운동 성격과 역할, 《군사軍史》 46, 2002

조풍연, 소파 방정환의 추억, 《신인간》 통권 389호, 신인간사, 1981

朴己煥, 近代日韓文化交流史研究-韓國人の日本留學, 大阪大學 大學院 文學研究科 博士論文, 1998

김민영, 사할린 땅에 버려진 한국인들, 《한국과 일본, 왜곡과 콤플렉스의 역사》 1, 자작나무, 1998

김성종, 사할린 한인동포 귀환과 정착의 정책과제, 《한국동북아논총》 40, 2006

편집부 엮음, 하와이 사진신부들, 《이야기 여성사》 1, 여성신문사, 1990

최안나, 하와이 이민 70년, 《신동아》 1974년 4월호

민찬, 단재 소설의 경로와 전통의 자장, 《단재 신채호의 현대적 조명》, 다운샘, 2003

정윤재, 단재 신채호의 국권회복을 향한 사상과 행동, 《단재 신채호의 현대적 조명》, 다운샘, 2003

박성수, 광복군과 임시정부, 《한국근대민족운동사》, 돌베개, 1980

곽건홍, 일제하 조선의 전시 노동정책 연구, 고려대 박사논문, 1998

박한용.장원정.황경, 남십자성 아래의 조선인들, 《시와 이야기가 있는 우리 역사》 2, 동녘, 1996

여순주, 일제말기 조선인 여자근로정신대에 관한 실태연구, 이화여대 석사논문, 1994

정용욱, 1945년말 1946년초 신탁통치 파동과 미군정-미군정의 여론공작을 중심으로, 《역사비평》 2003년 봄호

유영익, 이화장(梨花莊) 문서 속에 숨겨진 이승만의 참모습을 찾아서, 《한국사 시민강좌》 35, 2004

김보영, 정전회담 쟁점과 정전협정, 《역사비평》 2003 여름호

이란주, 어린 친구, 샤프라, 《아빠, 제발 잡히지 마》, 삶이 보이는 창, 2009

Catalogs

From the Daehan Empire to North-South rapprochement

Letters from Korean History
Volume V

First Published 5 May 2016
Third Published 10 April 2023

Author | Park Eunbong
Translator | Ben Jackson
Illustrator | Illustration: Park Jihoon, Map: Yu Sanghyeon

Design | Lee Seokwoon, Kim Miyeon

Published by | Cum Libro Inc. **CUM LIBRO 책과함께**
Address | 2F, Sowaso Bldg. 70, Donggyo-ro, Mapo-gu, Seoul, Korea 04022
Tel | (+82) 2-335-1982
Fax | (+82) 2-335-1316
E-mail | prpub@daum.net
Blog | blog.naver.com/prpub
Registered | 3 April 2003 No. 25100-2003-392

ISBN 979-11-86293-52-2 04740
ISBN 979-11-86293-46-1 (set)